What Brain Experts and Readers are Saying About the *INNERCISE*™ Book

Brain Experts

"Very few books can transform cutting-edge neuroscience into easy, practical strategies that will actually enhance the functioning of your brain in ways that will help you to master your thoughts and emotions so that you can achieve any goal you desire. *INNERCISE* does just that: Brilliant, powerful, and easy to apply to every part of your life!"

MARK WALDMAN, BRAIN RESEARCHER & EXECUTIVE MBA FACULTY, LOYOLA MARYMOUNT UNIVERSITY

"*INNERCISE* is an engaging, informed, and systematic guide to catalyze mind/brain self-discovery and transformation. John masterfully integrates and simplifies complex processes to help you train your brain for achieving greater success."

DAVID KRUEGER MD, PSYCHIATRIST, AUTHOR, & EXECUTIVE MENTOR COACH

"Only through daily *INNERCISE* can we create the sustainable habits necessary to transform the stress in our lives to fuel positive change."

HEIDI HANNA, PHD, NY TIMES BESTSELLING AUTHOR AND EXECUTIVE DIRECTOR OF THE AMERICAN INSTITUTE OF STRESS

"*INNERCISE* is a fantastic resource for anyone interested in taking their life to the next level. John Assaraf has taken complex neuroscience concepts and broken them down in such a way that they are not only easy to understand—more importantly, they are easy to apply. Readers will be thrilled with the practical roadmap John has laid out—a step-by-step approach to achieving the goals and creating the lives they dream about."

DR. JOAN ROSENBERG, PROFESSOR OF PSYCHOLOGY, PEPPERDINE UNIVERSITY, BESTSELLING AUTHOR OF EASE YOUR ANXIETY

"*INNERCISE* provides essential information and terrific brain training techniques for keeping your inner brain and outer mind focused on achieving your goals."

DR. ANDREW NEWBERG, NEUROSCIENTIST & AUTHOR OF HOW ENLIGHTENMENT CHANGES YOUR BRAIN

"John has a gift for making science accessible. In *INNERCISE*, he breaks down the practical steps with which you can transform your brain to achieve the results you want in your life!"

DANIEL FRIEDLAND MD, CEO OF SUPERSMARTHEALTH, AUTHOR OF LEADING WELL FROM WITHIN

"*INNERCISE* is filled with many tools you can use today to boost your brain."

DR. DANIEL AMEN, BRAIN EXPERT, FOUNDER OF AMEN CLINICS, & AUTHOR OF CHANGE YOUR BRAIN, CHANGE YOUR LIFE

"Cutting-edge techniques to maximize your fullest potential."

DR. SRINI PILLAY, HARVARD PSYCHIATRIST AND BRAIN EXPERT

"*INNERCISE* offers cutting edge techniques anyone can use to eliminate the hidden mental and emotional obstacles that keeps them from achieving their life's biggest goals and dreams. A MUST read."

DR. GEORGE PRATT, PHD CLINICAL PSYCHOLOGY

Readers & Listeners

"The knowledge contained in this book for the mere cost of around $15.00 is worth much more than a couple hundred dollars. Why you ask? Because it breaks things down into bite size categories and includes in each chapter a way to access as many bonuses as his $199.00 program! Each chapter is easily explained and defined so well that it leads you into each consecutive chapter and builds a great foundation for anyone to apply to anything one would encounter in life. I knew this book would be great but it surpassed all my expectations!"

C. PARKER

"Strengthen Your MINDSET. From managing your fears to decreasing your daily stress levels this book shows you how to create a positive mindset that will set you up for a successful life.

Your subconscious brain is vast and powerful and as you learn in this book - that is what needs to be INNERCISED AND RETRAINED simply using willpower does not work.

If you are tired of seeing the same results - over and over again - then I HIGHLY recommend you get this Book!"

STEVEN B.

"Simply put, everyone should read this book. Personally, I like to grab the physical copy and that Audible version so I can listen and follow along. It helps to internalize the information.

Chapter 6 alone is worth multiple times the price of the book because you will learn exactly how habits work, exactly what to do in order to stop bad habits, and exactly what to do in order to create new, positive habits. This alone could change everything for you.

I whole-heartedly recommend grabbing a copy of *INNERCISE*. You'll be glad you did."

THOMAS B.

"Very informative and mind opening! I loved the practical exercises and examples of *INNERCISE*. Being aware of what is going on in your brain is an empowering tool for life."

CHELSEY L. (AMAZON.COM CUSTOMER)

"Great listen. This book gives simple yet powerful concepts and the ways to retrain your brain and life!"

AMAZON.COM CUSTOMER

"I love this book. The knowledge I have gained from listening to this book is very powerful and I hope to utilize it to become the best human being that I can be."

"Great. Great book if only John narrated it, it could have had my 5 stars, other than that it's great I got through the book in a week 1 hour a day. The real life stories were a perfect touch and the extra training content is genius. I wish all self-improvement books had that option so even if you're having trouble with the *INNERCISE* training you can always go and get help properly."

"Amazing book!! This book is filled with knowledge! I loved every chapter and look forward to reading again. The insightful information is priceless."

INNERCISE

INNERCISE

*The New Science to **Unlock** Your Brain's Hidden Power*

John Assaraf

Waterside Press

Printed in the United States of America

First Printing, 2018
Second Printing, 2019
Third Printing, 2019
Fourth Printing, 2021
Fifth Printing, 2023

ISBN-13: 978-1-947637-82-5 print edition
ISBN-13: 978-1-947637-83-2 ebook edition

Waterside Productions
2055 Oxford Ave
Cardiff, CA 92007
waterside.com

"Whatever the mind can conceive and believe, it can achieve."

—Napoleon Hill

Contents

Foreword

When I first met John Assaraf, I was unsure about what to expect. I heard that he was a "self-help" guru who was interested in introducing the power of brain science to the world. The "self-help" world is inundated with people who claim to have expertise because they have suffered an adversity. They then seek to engage the empathy of others by creating a "community" of people to whom they can sell their products. I hoped that John didn't want to use my experience as a psychiatrist and brain researcher to validate that or some similar approach. And boy, was I pleasantly surprised!

Instead, what I found was a man who had a deep and profound understanding of the human condition, and a person who genuinely wanted to help people learn how to use their brains to navigate through their life challenges. Not only did he reach out to as many experts as possible to validate his findings, but in the process, he developed an ever-evolving sense of how the brain works. The result of these years of work is *Innercise*. I am proud to endorse this revolutionary message in the strongest possible way.

Innercise is one of the most comprehensive collections of brain-based approaches to achieving success and living a happier life. It is based on years of extensive research by some of the most distinguished scientists in the world. And it is the first book to explicitly open the door to the idea that, like exercise, we need to be "working out" our brains if we want to be psychologically strong and flexible.

While no scientist will lay claim to science being the only and ultimate truth, using a scientific method of engaging your brain provides a framework. It is a path forward to help you interact with your own brain, both consciously and unconsciously. John accurately points out that it is our unconscious processes that often dictate the results in our lives, and he demonstrates how you can access and change your brain to feel better, while getting tangible results too.

We are far from knowing the perfect way forward. Yet, *never before* has such a comprehensive compendium of exercises been created in a simple, research-based, and easy-to-understand way that can help you reach your goals.

The book is cutting-edge in its content, highlighting such ideas as the latest research in neuroplasticity (brain change), and how to accelerate this process. In the same way that exercising will help you build your muscles, Innercising will help you build your brain. John has outlined a way to do this, not just to sharpen your thinking, but to master your emotions and behaviors too. From managing fear to decreasing stress and creating a positive mindset, John provides just the tools you need to jump-start your brain. With these methods by your side, you can feel confident to address any challenge in life.

We are prone to being stuck in thought patterns in life. Self-sabotage is often our greatest enemy. In this book, John shows you how you can change brain blood flow using positive self-talk and many other proven techniques, to escape habit-hell. And he demonstrates that the benefits of understanding this new brain science are likely within your grasp.

The human brain is a beautiful and complex organ. It contains much of the programming that determines how we live our lives. Most people go through life as if they have been dealt a hand of cards that they have no control over. But John shows you that this is not the case. That your present and future life is in your hands. While there are no perfect and predictable solutions, there *are* ways in which you can make your life better. *Innercise* offers you a path forward to change your life.

Srini Pillay, MD
NeuroBusiness Group, CEO

Introduction

In the 1950s and '60s, Jack Lalanne revolutionized the physical fitness and health industry by promoting and teaching exercise and nutrition.

Today, we complete the fitness revolution with *Innercise*—a comprehensive guide to science-based mental and emotional techniques to strengthen your mind-set and unleash the hidden power of your brain.

Lack of knowledge or skill is not what really holds you back. It's your mind-set, emotional blocks, and deeply ingrained habits that you must release to clear the path to your greatest victories and successes. With *Innercise*, you'll learn to change your habitual patterns, and eliminate disempowering emotions like

- Fear of failure or success
- Shame and embarrassment
- Fear of being judged
- Low self-worth
- Negativity and pessimism
- Lack of confidence

Your limiting beliefs, stories, and excuses are nothing more than reinforced subconscious patterns that cause you to think, feel, and consistently behave in ways that produce the same results over and over again.

Now, cutting-edge technology and the science of neuroplasticity have finally unlocked the door to breaking free from these patterns. My hope in writing this book is that it will empower you to recognize and release whatever is holding you back from your fullest potential and the grandest vision for your life.

You will discover powerful, brain-based techniques that elite athletes, Navy SEALs, CEOs, and astronauts use to upgrade their awareness and skills, so they perform at the highest level possible. *Innercise* is your key to greater mental toughness, more confidence, and increased emotional fortitude. With it, you'll achieve your health, wealth, career, relationship, and business goals faster and easier than ever before.

To your amazing success,

John Assaraf
CEO, NeuroGym

Before You Begin

Innercise is not a brain "game" or a memory enhancer. The experiential steps and techniques you'll be guided through in this book are grounded in evidence-based research and the latest neuroscientific discoveries.

Innercising daily can help you strengthen your mindset and upgrade your emotional skills, so you can eliminate the obstacles that are holding you back from achieving your biggest goals and dreams.

Just like you can strengthen your physical muscles with exercise, it's helpful to think of your brain as having "neuro-muscles" that you can strengthen using Innercise.

Imagine that you want to strengthen your bicep muscle. You could exercise it by doing bicep curls or pushups. Similarly, using Innercises, you can train neuro-muscles such as your beliefs, willpower, habits, confidence, focus, and more. For physical training, you can do "sets" of bench presses and curls. For mental training, you can do "stacks" of affirmations, visualizations, and positive aromatic associations to name a few.

What does an Innercise look like? Here are just a few ways to strengthen your neuro-muscles:

- Mental contrasting
- Cognitive priming

- Guided hypnotic stories
- Anchoring techniques
- Meditation and mindfulness
- Guided brain training audios and videos
- Neurofeedback training
- Neural rescripting techniques

There are literally as many Innercises that you can do to strengthen your mindset and emotional skills as there are exercises to strengthen your muscles and internal organs. And with Innercise, you can train in the privacy of your own home or office, and on your smartphone, tablet, or computer.

Doing a variety of guided or self-directed Innercises daily will have a compounding, positive effect on your mindset, emotions, and behaviors. You'll be exposed to the scientifically proven power of neuroplasticity and neuropsychology to create new subconscious beliefs and habitual mental and emotional patterns that can serve as a foundation for you to achieve your greatest victories faster and easier than ever before.

As a part of this book, you also gain free access to some incredibly powerful audio and video training programs designed to help you transform your life from the inside out. Simply go to www.myneurogym.com/innercise.

In addition, throughout the book you will read about our free Brain-A-Thon training with me and other world renowned brain and success experts. You can sign up at www.innercisebook.com/brainathon

The Innercise Revolution

Over three decades ago, a very wise and successful man asked me a simple yet profound question that transformed my life. At the time, I was just nineteen years old, with no college behind me and none in front as far as I could see. I still had dreams of being successful, at least as I thought it to be: mansions, yachts, fancy cars, hot bodies, glamorous lives. Those things captivated me, and I was determined that one day I would become as financially successful as the people I saw on *Lifestyles of the Rich and Famous*.

There were, however, a few hiccups along the way to realizing my dreams.

The first was I had left high school about two years earlier, right after eleventh grade. The second, I was still living in my parents' apartment. I'd been told that, without a college degree, I was going to have to settle for working for minimum wage. I have to admit, that warning hit home. My father was living proof—as a cab driver he was always chasing down the next fare and barely made ends meet.

Worse, although I'd been working at one part-time job or another since I was eight, my work experience was patchy—I held different jobs, perhaps the longest-lasting one was a stint as a scrappy street kid shoplifting, committing petty crimes, and, due to my larger size compared to the other kids, a reliable brawler in street fights.

I had reached a turning point though that summer of my nineteenth year on earth. I looked back just long enough to say good-bye to the shore and cast my sights to the open waters in search of a better future.

As fate or God's will or whatever you want to call it showed up, I was fortunate to cross paths with a wise and successful man. My concept of success at that time was pretty shallow. However, today with hindsight, I see that he was indeed very successful, in ways I only came to appreciate as I dug deeper for meaning and purpose in my life.

Alan Brown was an astute and wealthy entrepreneur who was also a wise and generous philanthropist. He loved to help people achieve their dreams, especially those with a sparkle of passion and success in their eyes. Alan saw that sparkle in mine.

One April afternoon at lunch, Alan was eating a healthy salad as I was chowing down a burger and fries, when our casual talk moved onto new ground. As I shared more of my life story with Alan, he listened patiently for a while, but as soon as I began to complain about all the ways I had been wronged: no education, no money, no connections, no skills—

"John," he interrupted, "whatever happened in the past is totally irrelevant. The past is your history. The only thing that matters is what you choose and decide to do for yourself starting right now. Today! The past you can't change, but you can *choose* to change your future."

I was taken aback, filled with skepticism. A moment later though hope shined its light. "How can I do that? How do I choose my future?"

"By answering three simple yet very profound questions."

Those questions would change the direction of my life forever.

"What, specifically, do you want to achieve?" He was careful to point out that he was asking not what I thought I *could* achieve, but what I really *wanted to achieve*.

I shared with him some of my biggest goals and dreams, like retiring when I was forty-five with a net worth of three million dollars. How I would have a big home, a fancy sports car, and enough money to travel the world and take care of my parents.

He nodded understandingly. "*Why* must you achieve these goals?" He asked me to dig deeper and come up with as many reasons as I could because, as he explained, "You'll need that leverage over yourself for the times when you don't feel like doing what it is you need to do."

And then he threw the mother of all questions at me. Looking deep into my eyes again, almost as if peering into my soul, he asked: "Are you interested in, or are you *committed to*, achieving these goals and living the life of your dreams?"

"Uh…man. I don't…well, what's the difference?" I asked.

"If you're interested," he said, "you'll do what's convenient and what is easy. You'll come up with stories and excuses of why you can't. You'll allow your past or present circumstances to control what you think and do. If you're interested, you won't be willing to go through the discomfort of change yourself—because change is absolutely required if you are serious about breaking free from your current beliefs, habits, and results.

"If, however, you're committed, then you'll do whatever it takes. You'll take action in spite of your doubts and fears. If you're committed, you will upgrade your knowledge, your skills, and your belief system of what *is* possible for you to achieve. If you are serious and committed, you will choose to let go of anything that is holding you back. I can teach you how to strengthen your mindset. That's where you start and from there you move to making the internal shifts needed to overcome your mental and emotional obstacles. I can teach you this. I can teach you how to override your subconscious, unpleasant emotions, and the automatic limiting behaviors that keep you stuck.

A few heartbeats passed in silence.

"So," Alan said softly, "are you interested or are you committed?"

I was excited and scared.

"So?" he asked again softly.

Finally, I held out my hand to shake his. "I'm committed. Let's do this!"

It was that commitment, that single decision at age nineteen, that kick-started everything for me. It was at that moment that naïve intentions and grandiose dreams shifted to me, truly forging the life I wanted.

Using what Alan and a few other amazing mentors taught me, I went on to build five multimillion-dollar companies. I've authored two New York Times bestselling books. I've been in eight movies and documentaries. I've been on national TV—*Larry King Live, The Ellen DeGeneres Show, CNN with Anderson Cooper,* and more.

I've created a life that not only resembles the people I watched on the *Lifestyles of the Rich and Famous,* but more important than all of that glamour, I have been enriched far beyond with excellent health, an incredible wife, and two amazing sons.

Don't let me mislead you though. This didn't all happen in a straight line. In fact, I've had as many steps backward and sideways as I've had going forward. It was not suddenly "happily ever after." Along with my material success, came an overindulgence in what were supposed to be heavenly rewards but, in reality, were hellish trappings. The result: two divorces. Alcohol and sugar addiction. Ulcerative colitis. Prediabetes. Stock market busts. A business bankruptcy and more than 50 extra pounds of fat that my body didn't need. My life in the fast lane cost me my health, dear loves and friendships, millions of dollars, and very nearly my sanity.

In the end, the Innercises and guidance in this book are what helped me turn my setbacks into my biggest comebacks *by being committed to achieving the life of my dreams… no matter what.*

You Can Make the Same Commitment

By now, some thirty-seven years since that conversation with Alan, I've asked those same three questions to tens of thousands of my students. *There's magic in those questions.* They can be the gateway to an entirely new life for you.

Innercise is a book about using your brain to achieve your goals and dreams. It's a practical, science-based guide to understanding what holds you back, and what can lead you forward. In the pages that follow:

- You'll be introduced to empowering ways that can transform your life.

- You'll learn how to recognize and release feelings of uncertainty and doubt that cause you to procrastinate and deny taking the right steps toward achieving spiritual, emotional, mental, and physical success.

- You'll learn to identify what's really holding you back and then reframing and releasing it, followed by retraining your brain to have the confidence, certainty, and focus to achieve your goals and dreams.

- You'll learn to feel, think, and act at your highest level so you can start to *achieve* your goals instead of just *setting* them.

- You'll learn how to live your life with more purpose and meaning: to feel in more control, freed from stress, circumstances, and people draining your vitality and energy.

We stand at the forefront of a revolution in brain science that can provide you with better tools to work more productively with far greater emotional and spiritual balance—a revolution that can help you create a life filled with deeper meaning, passion, purpose, and joy.

So, ask yourself this question: Are you merely *interested* in having the life you desire, or are you *committed* to having it?

PART I:

Know Thy Brain

"What I am looking for is not out there, it is in me."

—Helen Keller

It's Not Your Fault

Why Reaching Your Goals Has Been So Hard

"Those who cannot change their minds cannot change anything."

—George Bernard Shaw

Picture a grain of sand.

Can you see it? Let me help. It's about the size of this period below:

Now, imagine that instead of being a grain of sand, this dot is actually a *tiny piece of your brain*. Just a little speck of what we call "gray matter." If you could look closely enough, first, you'd discover this dot is actually made up of special nerve cells called *neurons*—and this tiny speck of brain, the one that's the size of a grain of sand, *can contain as many as 100,000 of these neurons.*

Look even closer.

These neurons are "talking" to each other, sending signals across connections called *synapses*. There can be up to a *billion* connections in that tiny speck alone. A billion!

Now, step back.

Zoom out and see that instead of one dot, you have thousands upon thousands of these dots accumulating into *billions* of neurons and *trillions* of connections.

These numbers—billions, trillions—are mind-bending in scope. Taken in totality, they make your brain one of the most complex life forms in the known universe. Many think of this like it's no big deal, if they think of it at all.

But this three-pound miracle *is* a big deal. Your brain does a staggering amount of work: It runs all your organs and regulates your temperature; it operates your immune system; it repairs the constant damage done to your body. It also controls your muscles and runs your digestive system. It keeps your heart beating, your eyes moving, your hair growing. It warns you of danger and fights cancer and welcomes in love and pleasure.

And that's still just scratching the surface. There is faith, consciousness, instinct, and so much more. It does all of this while you drive a car, think about that Great American Novel you want to write, and talk through a challenging problem with someone you trust.

Everything. From tiny to huge, from the mundane to the epic, your brain does it all; and it does so with a complexity and mysterious elegance that the most dedicated scientists in the world have yet to even begin to understand.

Every moment of brilliant genius, breathtaking creativity, and astonishing accomplishment in human history was accomplished with an evolving brain made up of stuff *like yours*. The Fortune 500 CEO's brain? Same stuff. The coworker who lost all that weight? The friend who quit her job and started a successful business? Lincoln's brain? Einstein's brain? *Same stuff.* Of course, there are differences; some people have regions with greater amounts of creativity, or intellect, or empathy. And brain chemistry varies. DNA varies. But still, our brains are made of the same stuff; or as neuroscientists would say, of a "consistent molecular architecture."

I imagine many of you are shaking your heads right now questioning: *Really? Well, if my brain is so powerful, why do I have so much trouble achieving what I want?*

The answer will amaze you.

Setting Goals versus Achieving Goals

Think for a moment about the last time you set a goal. I'm not referring to cutting the grass or doing your taxes, but something much larger and more important. Something that would add the greater purpose and meaning you yearn for.

Perhaps you want to start a business. Or earn more income. Fall in love. Feel better about yourself. Whatever your goal, if it is *important* to you, then there's a good chance something will eventually happen: *you will fall short*. Don't get me wrong. I'm an eternal optimist. You give me lemons and I'll find a way to make lemonade. It's not just a positive attitude—I know plenty of "can do" people who find out they can't do. It's not just about talent—mediocrity is often rewarded in business and government, particularly when flash is more appealing than substance. And it's not just about hard work—new business owners reportedly work an average of 60 to 80 hours a week, often with only a minimal paycheck coming in, yet 80 percent of startups don't survive past 36 months.

Clearly attitude, talent, and a strong work ethic are critical. But most of our big goals are not achieved because we set ourselves up to fail. Just look at the statistics for those who try to lose weight. Or at the high percentage of troubled marriages. Better yet, don't rely on statistics from some big university study; ask your friends how they fared with their New Year resolutions.

All this underscores the thinking that *achieving goals is hard.*

But wait. Is this true?

Think about it. How often have you imagined yourself richer, thinner, or happier? More connected, better liked? Kinder? More generous? Think of the times you've wanted a shiny new car, a promotion, or a date with the amazing person you just met. Defining your goals can come to you as naturally as eating and sleeping. In fact, one of the great marvels of the modern human brain is we have the capacity to look toward the future with an effortless grace. So, when it comes to setting goals, that's anything *but* hard. We are, in many ways, goal-desiring and goal-setting machines!

That's not the trouble. But *reaching* them can be. It's in taking action and moving toward our goals consistently even when things go awry, as they almost certainly will.

In one moment, we might be filled with the rush of neurotransmitters like dopamine, serotonin, or endorphins—all which make us feel motivated, energetic, confident… and the next thing we know we haven't even gotten off the couch and dove in to what needs to be done. Or maybe we do get going, filled with energy and good intentions like when we kick off the New Year with a new exercise and diet plan. But somewhere along the way we lose our mojo, we drift, almost imperceptibly at times right back to where we started.

Why is it so hard to accomplish what we set out to do?

Your Brain's Two Priorities

Take heart. It's more complicated than you think as to why your workouts trailed off, or why you couldn't come up with a clear picture of who your target market would be for your dream business.

Yes, your brain is amazing. But it's also a work-in-progress. From the earliest known human ancestors living some seven million years ago to today, our brains have slowly, steadily, transformed. And continue to.

For that transformation to be possible—to get from hominid brain to *your* brain—the organ evolved under two important principles.

The first is safety. More than anything, brains need to survive. In order to live long enough to reproduce and pass brain improvements on to the next generation, brains cannot die too soon. That means your brain has naturally evolved to keep you safe—emotionally, physically, and mentally.

The second is efficiency. Remember that long list of jobs your brain is taking control of, from blinking your eyes to thinking analytically? The only way to get all that done is to be efficient with energy. Your brain has to focus on energy conservation so that it can do more with less.

These two factors had a distinct effect on how the brain you have today works. From running from the jaws of a saber-toothed tiger to swerving around a distracted driver, your brain has evolved instinctual, automatic reactions to make sure you move out of harm's way. To be efficient, rather than learn from scratch new habits for every single thought, emotion, and action, your brain instead relies on familiar behaviors that can be implemented with very little energy.

Safety and efficiency help you survive, but they don't ensure you will *thrive*.

Your Autopilot Life

Those ultrafast responses—the instincts and automated ways of thinking, feeling, and acting that serve so well to keep you alive and running efficiently—come with a cost though. They run most of your life and thus in many ways you are more or less a collection of habits, many of which you're barely aware of. Your life, in other words, is largely on autopilot. This is called automaticity and **it's why you keep getting results you don't like; not once, not twice, but over and over again. When you think, feel, and act the same way, when you are habituated to stay the same way, your life turns out more or less the same way too.**

Change Threatens the Brain

Survival is an issue for all life forms. Every living organism adapts, or evolves, to meet changing threats, environments, needs. There are very rare exceptions; for instance, sulfur bacteria found off the coast of Western Australia show no evidence of having evolved in nearly 2 billion years. But we humans are definitely not among these rarities. In fact, we have evolved substantially. Our brains are now three times larger than our earliest ancestors, and the shapes of our brains have changed too in accommodating learning language, analytical thinking, consciousness, cultural and technological advances and more.

Yet, *your brain* hasn't adapted well in some fundamental ways too. My friend Dr. Adam Gazzaley, a neuroscience professor at the University of California, San Francisco, says we are all burdened with ancient brains trying to focus and survive in a high-tech world.

Here's an example of what Adam means: Your goal to lose weight might seem exciting and inspiring to you, but your ancient brain wants you to keep that weight on in case there's a famine around the corner. Or, the idea of leaving your job to start a business might send a tingle of excitement down your spine, but your ancient brain "worries" that the loss of your current job and income could lead to starvation.

To your brain, almost any change you want to make is interpreted as a potential *risk*—emotionally, financially, physically, mentally, socially. And the mother of them all, a risk perceived as potentially one that could kill you.

All of this leads us to the same quandary every time. Setting goals isn't hard. *Achieving* them is hard because, as far as your brain is concerned, radical change is a potential threat.

When we look at change this way, we begin to see the light at the end of a very dark tunnel. In your own life, this may show up as glimpses of answers to some nagging questions like these:

- Why do I keep starting to change, and end up right back where I started?

- Why is it so hard to break the thought patterns I have? The emotional patterns? The behavior patterns?

- Why do I get stuck earning the same income?

- Why is it so hard to leave a job or relationship that is no longer satisfying and rewarding?

- Why do I continually sabotage myself with every diet I try?

And perhaps the most nagging one of all:

Why can't I seem to complete the goals that would bring me what I want?

The answer to each is the same. *Significant change, for the brain, feels like a significant threat, and it will do everything possible to resist leaving its "comfort zone."*

Consider the thermostat in your home. It keeps the temperature the same, no matter if it's hot or cold outside. If you open a window in the winter to let in some fresh air, the thermostat registers the change, and turns the heat on, bringing your home back to "normal" so that you'll feel safe and snug.

Your mental and emotional habits of a lifetime have set the "temperature" at a certain point, too. So, you're comfortable within a certain range of feelings, behaviors, and thoughts. But when you try to change the way you feel or think or act—to open a window to let in some fresh air—the "thermostat" in your brain kicks in to bring you right back to what it has come to be known as your "normal" comfort zone. The result is you stay stuck, or maybe embattled with yourself to eke out slow incremental gains instead of the giant steps you envisioned.

Yet some people do manage to override this resistance and achieve change. They lose weight and keep it off, they start businesses that fuel them, they get promoted, they earn more, they have loving and fulfilling relationships, they find true *happiness*, they write a book and take dancing lessons. They thrive, not just survive.

And, so can you. But to do this, you have to understand that you have not one brain, but two.

Chapter Summary and Resources

Summary

- Your brain is an astonishingly complex and powerful organ. But for all that power, reaching your goals can seem impossible at times.

- Your brain has evolved greatly to keep you safe and running efficiently, but priorities are different now than they were seven million ago. Your brain though is still a work in progress and often struggles to keep up with the changes needed to meet your new priorities. Actually, old habits and automated ways of thinking, feeling, and acting can keep you stuck.

Additional Free Resources

If you want additional help and free resources on how to best use each section in the book, I'm including some special coaching videos and 9 mini brain-training audios to go along with the book. I will act as your mindset coach as part of buying Innercise. For now, get started with this book and the free resources. Just scan the code below on your smartphone and log in to the NeuroGym platform or go to www.myneurogym.com/innercise to create a log in so you gain access to the free bonuses and resources.

Meet the Gorilla

How Your Two Brains Are Keeping You Stuck

"Two things are infinite: the universe and human stupidity; and I'm not sure about the universe."

—Albert Einstein

It's likely you can fairly easily recall times in the past when you felt confident, or perhaps you're feeling good about yourself now. Either way, reflect more deeply on this confidence, and you will also get even clearer pictures of things you're proud of, things you've accomplished, whether large or small.

But I'm also willing to bet that you can think of the times when you've felt stuck. The times when you did your research, read books, and attended motivational seminars, but no matter how hard you worked, you just couldn't seem to break through to make serious gains in your current income, your business, your health, your relationships, your spiritual development or other goals. Sure, you'd continue to set new goals—maybe even affirm them, visualize them, set intentions toward them—but still, just weren't able to reach them.

We know the first part of why not: Your brain has evolved to keep you safe and in your comfort zone by creating neural patterns that become habits. Those habitual thought and emotional patterns make a huge impact on the life you have.

A Tale of Two "Brains"

The habitual patterns that your brain uses to be efficient have another distinctive characteristic: *they run below the level of your awareness.* They're what we call *nonconscious*, or *subconscious*, and they reveal one very important fact:

You have two "brains," not one.

Not two brains in the physical sense, of course, but neuroscience has shown that one part of your brain is your rational, logical, conscious mind, while the majority of the other areas operate in a much deeper emotional and habitual way that is largely controlled by your limbic, ancient, subconscious mind.

Your Conscious Brain	Your Subconscious Brain
Super slow	Lightning fast
Conceptual	Perceptual
Thoughts and feelings	Instincts and emotions
Deliberate	Habitual
Explicit	Implicit

The conscious/subconscious divide explains so much of why change is difficult. You might consciously want to have more intimate relationships, for example, but subconsciously you are anchored to protecting yourself from feeling rejected. Or similarly, you might consciously want to lose weight but subconsciously fear that even if you were thinner you still might feel unlovable, so why bother.

And therein lies the problem: While you may *choose* your goals consciously, your thoughts often conflict with your hidden emotions and instincts. You can set goals consciously, but if your subconscious processing, habits, and old conditioning are working against you, change becomes difficult, if not impossible.

Meet the 800-Pound Gorilla

Not only do you have two different brains, they are unequal. First of all, **almost *all* of what goes on in your brain registers in your subconscious.** That's right. The vast majority of the activity going on in your brain, right now, is happening beneath the level of your awareness.

It's a bit disconcerting at first. We like to think that our conscious mind is in charge. That we're the captain of our ship and our mind and body do what we consciously tell them to. Nobody disputes that our brain has some autopilot systems to help with keeping our heart beating, keeping our lungs breathing, and generally keeping the lights on, but we really want to believe—I mean really want to believe just as sure as the sun will rise each morning—that we are at the controls with our deliberate, rational, logical conscious self.

When in fact, it's more the opposite. Your conscious/subconscious ratio is like an iceberg where your conscious brain activity is the tiny part above the surface, and your subconscious is submerged fathoms deep. To put some numbers to this image, the general consensus among most neuroscientists is that only about three to five percent of what's happening in your brain occurs at the conscious level of awareness. The other 95 to 97 percent happens in the vast hidden beneath.

The imbalance doesn't end there though. Your subconscious brain is lightning fast. It can sense and react to a potential threat before your conscious brain can even get its pants on, and that gives it a kind of VIP status in your mind.

All told, this makes your subconscious brain like the proverbial 800-pound gorilla in the room. And, as the joke goes, what do you give an 800-pound gorilla? Anything it wants.

In this case, what the gorilla wants more than anything is something called *coherence.*

Getting the Band Back Together: Coherence vs. Dissonance

You may not realize it, but if you've ever been to a classical music performance, you've witnessed an example of how your brain operates at its most efficient level.

Each instrument in the orchestra has a part to play. The patterns of music that each part plays are carefully arranged to complement each other. When the parts are played well, the frequencies of the different notes fit together in such pleasing synergy, the beautiful music you hear is sensed as enlightened oneness.

But when the parts are played *inharmoniously,* the whole arrangement can turn sour. False notes create discord. Senses become chaotic. And if the misaligned instrument isn't brought back into the fold, the whole piece can collapse into a noisy mess.

Your brain works like an orchestra—one that *plays well enough together* so that when you follow habits and think and act in alignment with your belief patterns and emotions, you can play some decent music. We call this *coherence*. For the brain, coherence represents the ideal state of safety and efficiency, the two priorities we looked at earlier. When your brain is in coherence, it thinks all is well, there's music, and the gorilla is happy.

However, if you try to think or behave differently in ways that don't make the gorilla happy, the music stops, and you introduce *dissonance*. For example, when you try to change your eating habits, or take the risk of starting a business, or admit your mistake and apologize to your significant other, you might be deviating from the old, comfortable, habitual script you've been relying on for a lifetime. You might want to start creating new patterns with healthier habits instead of sticking with the standard behavior that you've learned. And that's *not* what the gorilla wants. Dissonance is metabolically expensive. It takes energy. There's a "switch cost" to making change, and since your brain doesn't like to waste energy, it will work to restore coherence.

If your emotional desires, and innermost values and habits, don't align with your rational goals and mindset, the motivational circuits and decision-making "CEO" inside your brain become like an orchestra with too much trombone. Your efforts to get what you want will be compromised, and your ability to achieve your goals will be crippled. Period.

The gorilla will demand the orchestra get back to coherence and back to what is familiar and comfortable.

Dissonance is exhausting—both for your brain, and for *you.* If your two brains are in a constant state of neural dissonance, always fighting each other and undermining your ability to succeed at anything, it's like having one foot on the gas and one foot on the brake. It's not only tiring—it's extremely frustrating!

How to Recognize Neural Dissonance

- Lack of organization
- Mood swings
- Lack of personal peace
- Overwhelm
- Confusion
- Lack of energy
- Self-doubt
- Worry and stress
- Fear and anxiety
- Excuses
- Excessive procrastination
- Mind-wandering and chaotic thinking
- Lack of confidence
- Lack of focus

How to Recognize Neural Coherence

- Peak performance
- Being in flow
- Feeling organized and comfortable
- Clear, focused thinking

- Reduced stress and a feeling of calmness
- A sense of being emotionally grounded
- Enhanced happiness and well-being
- Increased confidence and certainty

What Gorilla Wants…Gorilla Gets

Of course, we like to think that we can override all of this. We think we can overpower the gorilla and muscle our way to success. In fact, we have a whole toolbox of *conscious* brain techniques that try to do just that:

Willpower? Sure, you can wrestle the gorilla. But for how long?

Goal-setting? Sure, you can tell the gorilla what you want, but the gorilla doesn't have to listen.

Plans? Sure. Make your plans. But don't expect the gorilla to *follow them.*

But you simply cannot override millions of years of evolution. You can't muscle through or out-clever the power of your thought and behavioral patterns you've been building on since birth. Every time you try to change, your subconscious brain, your gorilla, is going to try like hell to bring you back to the status quo in its thinking that this is where you need to be for your own safety and efficiency. In the face of this, you'll probably start to rationalize why you shouldn't go looking for trouble. You might think, *Is this really a good idea? Do I really want this? Is it even possible? Do I even deserve it?*

This is why goal-setting and goal-achieving are such different things, and why you can end up stuck. When you try to change, you're out of alignment with your subconscious brain. Goal setting is conscious.

But goal achievement? Not so much. So, unless your goals involve staying safe, and doing the same, comfortable, familiar things day after day—regardless of whether they make you miserable—*your gorilla is not going to be on board to help you.*

That's why the newest scientific research shows that trying harder and working longer is not the key to transforming your life. Of course, a strong work ethic is a virtue, but as this research shows there are limits, and ignoring those limits can lead to physical and emotional burnout. That's part of the picture. Another is if you don't find ways to tame your gorilla—to shift that evolutionary instinctual and emotional wiring toward joining you to transcend survival and upgrade to thriving—your success will be painfully limited.

That means you need a new approach.

The Solution: Train Your Brain with Innercise

This is where we've landed: While motivational strategies and positive thinking can affect the conscious or logical part of your brain, it's your subconscious, emotional, and instinctual brain that predominately drives your behaviors. Meaning, to break free from where you are and to get to where you want to be, you must retrain your subconscious mind to be in agreement with your conscious mind and goals.

The good news is brain scan studies show that you can change and strengthen the key areas in your brain that control your conscious and subconscious nature. It largely requires applying right-brain training methodologies and technologies that can help rescript and reshape your self-image and your self-confidence and help reset many of the unproductive perceptions and mental and emotional habits that drive your daily behavior.

Enter *Innercises*—science-based techniques that help you unlock your brain's hidden powers, so you can take inspired action to achieve your goals faster and easier than ever before.

As you continue through the book, you'll find many Innercises—some just take a few moments to complete. Each one is like an exercise for your brain. Repeat them and combine them in what we call stacks just as you would physical exercise sets in a gym.

And like physical exercises, Innercises work best when you don't overdo it and instead listen to your body. In fact, please don't even think about doing *all* of your Innercise in one day. For best results, use *spaced repetition*—complete your Innercises, then leave some time for your brain to incorporate what you've experienced. When it feels right, then go at it again.

Innercises fall into seven basic categories:

1. Self-Esteem/Self-Worth/Self-Image
2. Beliefs, Perceptions, Perspectives
3. Habits and Behaviors
4. Focus/Concentration

5. Stress Reduction and Relaxation

6. Gratitude and Pleasure

7. Overcoming Fears, Stories, and Excuses

Let's get the ball rolling with this simple foundational Innercise:

It's called "Take 6: Calm the Circuits," and you can do it anytime in just sixty seconds. Whenever you are feeling stressed, anxious, or even fearful, start with Take 6.

. . . .

INNERCISE: "TAKE 6: Calm the Circuits"

Do this now:

Take six deep rhythmic breaths in through your nose and out through your mouth, like you are blowing out of a straw. As you breathe in, say,

> *I breathe in calmness, I breathe out stress.*
>
> *or*
>
> *I breathe in calmness, I breathe out fear.*
>
> *or*
>
> I breathe in calmness, I breathe out anxiety, or overwhelm.

. . . .

Research has shown that when you are under mental, emotional, or even financial duress, your stress center is activated, which in turn lowers your brain's executive function abilities.

Taking six rhythmic breaths helps to deactivate your stress response system and allows you to be in a calm and proactive mind frame versus a disempowered and reactive one. Being calm is essential to freeing yourself from the neural patterns locking you up in your mental or emotional prison.

It's Time to Break Out of Your Mental Prison!

Being stuck is deeply uncomfortable. You're able to see out, but you're not able to get out to the life you know is there waiting for you. Yet, instead of finding ways to break free, many people opt to just soothe their discomfort by creating stories or making excuses. They "rational-lies," "Sure, I'm unhappy and I don't like it. But I'll make the best of it."

The truth is we all do this to varying degrees. *I just need more time. Things will get better. God is looking over me.* So, we live above our means. We pretend to be happy. We surround ourselves with distractions to forget about just how off-purpose we are. If you haven't already found out, you will—it doesn't work.

The good news is there are proven, effective methods that do work. Ones that can take with you wherever you go in the world in pursuit of your ambitions. It starts with understanding how your brain can be changed using remarkable breakthroughs in science and how you can apply that understanding to seize the day.

Real People. Real Results.

At eighty-six years old, Katrama was still dealing with past childhood challenges that she wanted to release; she still felt like she didn't belong and didn't deserve happiness.

At the tender age of two, Katrama and her family barely escaped the Nazi holocaust in Austria and fled to China. Nine years later, after enduring the bombings and deprivations of World War II, she was again forced to flee.

After several turbulent years, she was finally able to immigrate to the United States and settle peacefully in Los Angeles. Upon graduating high school, she went on to art schools in Los Angeles and Paris. Her search for meaning and making sense of life's twists and turns took many years. She always seemed to be looking for something new and exciting to keep herself busy and to earn an income.

Eventually, along with her husband, she created a destination wedding company that saw some success, but, like so many people, after the economy crashed, her decreased by 65 percent. They worked tirelessly to get the business up again but being in her eighties she recalls that "it was very tiring and discouraging and I could not find a way to get my enthusiasm or motivation going or to come up with a plan with new goals." The up and down pattern continued and she seriously considered throwing in the towel and selling or closing the business. She had no inspiration about what to do next.

Katrama committed herself Innercising daily and made it a habit to listen to the Innercise brain training audios for earning more money every morning. She knew she needed to overcome the old limiting beliefs that were holding her back. One by one, she worked on deleting her inhibiting thoughts of "I'm too old to start over" and replacing it with "I think, feel, and act young because I am."

Soon, she noticed a huge mental and emotional shift. "I recognized a new way to view life, to boost my energy and confidence to set goals, use new strategies, stay positive, and transform arising doubts." Not too long after, her business phones started buzzing with inquiries and bookings came in. She booked ten weddings for the upcoming month, which was more than double her usual monthly bookings. She invested more money in advertising and started asking clients for reviews, which she never dared to do before. She ended up earning over $245,000 and that allowed her to plan and pay for a three-week vacation to Thailand with her husband. She said, "At eighty years of age, I feel like forty-five again! I was able to change my beliefs, relationships, manifestation skills, posture, physiology, and, of course, daily rhythm and routines. These changes kept me feeling, looking, and becoming younger every day. This new confident outlook and lifestyle are inspiring me to live life to its fullest, no matter what obstacles arise. I feel bigger, stronger, and I now face my obstacles head on, delighting in knowing that I can overcome them."

Chapter Summary and Resources

Summary

- You have two "brains," not one. One that you're aware of (your conscious brain), and one that lives beneath your awareness (your subconscious brain).

- The vast majority of activity in your brain is subconscious.

- Your subconscious brain is fast and powerful. Simply using more willpower, hard work, or cleverness isn't enough to overcome "the gorilla."

- To achieve your highest potential, you need to align your conscious and subconscious brains.

- Your behavior and a majority of results are driven by your subconscious patterns, not your conscious choices.

Additional Free Resources

If you want additional help and free resources on how to best use each section in the book, I'm including some special coaching videos and 9 mini brain-training audios to go along with the book. I will act as your mindset coach as part of buying Innercise. For now, get started with this book and the free resources. Just scan the code below on your smartphone and log in to the NeuroGym platform or go to www.myneurogym.com/innercise to create a log in so you gain access to the free bonuses and resources.

Upgrading to Brain 2.0

Using Innercise to Flip the Neuroplasticity Switch

"Any man could, if he were so inclined, be the sculptor of his own brain."

—Santiago Ramón y Cajal, Spanish neuroanatomist
and Nobel Laureate

Without aligning your conscious and subconscious brains, you're not just fighting an uphill battle, you're fighting a heartbreaking one. To be clear, there are no physical divisions to make two brains: You don't have a *conscious lobe* or a *subconscious lobe*. Just the opposite. Your conscious and subconscious processes run on similar platforms of connected neurons. But what Innercise gives you is the ability to *change* that system: to build new neural connections that can *align your thoughts, emotions, and behaviors with what you ultimately want to achieve.*

Compare this to some of today's exceptional athletes, musicians, astronauts, military specialists, or anyone with access to the highest paid psychologists, therapists, and neuro-coaches. They help them hack into their own brain to break free from any mental or emotional obstacle that interferes with achieving their goals.

With Innercise, you can become an elite performer and train your brain, without having to spend a fortune. You can learn and practice the Innercises found in this book, as well as discover other brain-training programs by visiting www. MyNeuroGym.com. To understand the process more, let's go back inside your brain and get to know it a little better.

The Map of Your Mind

Instead of just imagining a 3-pound, wrinkled sponge that you call your brain, imagine for a moment that we *unfold* your brain, the way you might unfold a map.

Your "brain map" is populated with some 85 billion neurons so small that they are only visible with the aid of a super-powerful microscope. And just as people in close proximity will often have conversations, neurons often "talk" to each other too by using synapses and neurotransmitters. A synapse is an electrochemical bridge between neurons in the brain—the tiniest of trails connecting one neuron to another.

If we scan your whole brain map, we can see neurons of different sizes everywhere, and even the places where neurons are actively exchanging information. When neurons connect together, we can start to see something that might look like a get-together. So, you can see "tiny villages" with a few active conversations, "towns" with more clusters, and "big cities" with lots of crosstalk.

You'll also notice on your brain map that these groupings of neurons can be connected to other groupings by synapses—

some like a quiet ferry ride between San Francisco and Sausalito while others like Interstate-90 jammed with traffic from Chicago to Boston.

The synapses are different sizes because the more often neurons communicate with each other through a particular pathway, the wider and better their pathway gets. Foot trails can become highways with lots of use, while diminished use can end up as closed roads.

This connection between brain cells, and clusters of brain cells, is the basic unit of brain function. Every time you think, feel, act, or remember, you access or create patterns of connections involving a multitude of neurons. There are neural patterns for everything from brushing your teeth to speaking, and if you could see your brain map in action, you'd see your villages, towns, and cities of every size—innumerable clusters of neurons—connecting and communicating through a network of synapses. The myriad patterns in which they connect and communicate demonstrate your brain at work.

Hungry? That's a pattern firing in your brain. Deciding what to eat? That's another series of brain patterns. Reaching to open the fridge? Another series of patterns. Angry? Ashamed? Happy? Every thought, feeling, and action in your life is some combination of neural patterns connecting to one another.

Neuroplasticity: Your Secret Weapon for Change

Before the 1960s, the prevailing science said that you were hardwired at birth. And by the end of your childhood, the story went, your brain was more or less like a completed house: the foundation cemented, rooms built, roof nailed down. Maybe you could repaint the kitchen, but there was no way anyone was going to renovate.

Happily, those ideas turned out to be wrong. And instead the science of neuroplasticity has been widely accepted for about the last 10 years—your brain really *can* be renovated, and it can happen at *any* time. When you learn a new skill, you change your brain by making new neural connections. When you learn to play an instrument, speak a new language, juggle a ball, go for a walk, eat wild salmon, and so much more, *your brain begins to change.*

What's even more exciting, though, is that you can change your brain, not just by doing, but also just by *thinking*. For example, research shows that the act of *focusing and being aware* through meditation changes the brain too!

Exercise changes your brain. Diet changes your brain. Relaxation changes your brain. Daydreaming changes your brain. Reading changes your brain. Reading this book right now is changing your brain. And every powerful negative or positive thought or emotion that you concentrate on changes your brain in healthy or unhealthy ways too.

Neuroplasticity defines the brain's ability to change itself. It's what Innercise is based on, and it's the natural ability that you're going to be using to help you reach your goals.

Changing the Map: The Three Ways Neuroplasticity Works

Through Innercise, you can use the same principle that built your map—neurons firing and wiring together to reshape your brain. Innercise can steer this firing and wiring. That in turn can change how you think, feel, and act—both consciously *and* unconsciously. And that means you can optimize all the parts of your brain—even the gorilla—and align them for a more enjoyable and meaningful life.

There are three ways that neuroplasticity can alter the map of your mind:

1. *Neurogenesis:* More Places on the Map

Neurogenesis is the process of making more neurons, or brain cells. Creating more neurons means you have more of what is loosely called "gray matter." In the adult brain, this happens in key areas like the *hippocampus* as you learn something new.

2. *Hebb's Rule:* More and Bigger Roads

There's a saying in neuroscience: Neurons that fire together, wire together. It's based on what is known as Hebb's rule, and postulates that neurons that communicate with each other electrochemically create a bond, or path. When neurons connect repeatedly, that path gets stronger, creating a bigger, easier road to travel. As you work through the Innercises, you'll be doing two things: creating new roads that serve you better and pushing roads that don't too slowly deteriorate.

3. *Myelin:* Better Roads

Not only can you make more neurons and connect more of them in an enormous number of combinations, evidence also suggests you can improve how well the connections actually work.[1] This can happen with the addition of more *myelin*, a fatty sheath that surrounds different parts of certain neurons. Fatty myelin is often called the "white matter" of the brain, and it's thought to improve the function of neurons.

More neurons. More connections. Better connections. With those three things, and the discipline of Innercise, you exponentially increase the possibilities to transform your life. As an adult, some of your neuroplasticity is, in Innercise terms, turned *off*. But the good news is you can turn it back on.[2]

New Tricks for Old Dogs: Using Innercise to Flip on Your Neuroplasticity Switch

In the first few years of life, the brain is growing at an incredible rate. It's forming new neural connections almost constantly, and that uses up a lot of your precious energy. It's one reason why babies sleep so much. As you age though, your neuroplasticity slows down as new memories and skills are formed; habits begin to direct a lot of your daily activities, and new ideas get pushed aside.

In Innercise, we think of this as "flipping the switch" on neuroplasticity. As a child, your switch was mainly "on" in virtually every part of your brain. But as you grow up, some learning processes, beliefs, and behaviors became "fixed" in the circuitry of your brain; meaning the plasticity switch is stuck in the "mostly off" position to varying degrees in each individual. So, you might find one person so set in their ways that to try to get them to see a different viewpoint is like talking to a brick wall. Whereas a person who is more flexible can at least be reasoned with to weigh all sides of a new position, even if, ultimately, they end up agreeing only somewhat or possibly not all. Since we now know that neuroplasticity can work at *any* age, that brick wall of a person has no real basis for being that way. They're not old dogs who can't learn new tricks, they're just uninformed about how to flip the switch back on, or just unwilling to. The only thing holding them back is—right, you guessed it—themselves.

It is true that all Innercises can contribute to creating new patterns in your brain, but there are a few standouts that can particularly help flip on your neuroplasticity switch.

1. Novelty and Curiosity

Your brain loves novelty. From an evolutionary perspective, novelty has meant one of two things: danger or reward. *Is that sound in the brush something I could eat, or something that could eat me?* The answer has been critical to survival, and those with brains that paid attention to novelty and could tell the difference between a danger and a reward won. Those that couldn't, died off. The winners not only survived they also reproduced. And as a result, millions of years later, here we are with brains that *love* the rewards of novelty.

Novelty does a host of things for your brain. The learning centers in your brain—especially the *hippocampus* and amygdala—are associated with memory and they, along with other areas in your frontal and insular lobes, function as "novelty detectors." These areas compare new information coming through your senses, perceptions, and creative thoughts with older information stored in memory. When something new, interesting, and potentially pleasurable or rewarding shows up, your detectors trigger the release of neurochemicals, including *dopamine*.

Dopamine helps you get motivated, plan, and prioritize. It also helps you form new memories and create new habits. There's a whole lot of science about dopamine—nicknamed a "happiness hormone," along with its cousins, endorphins and serotonin—but in short, it stimulates new neural activity; activity that is triggered by novelty—even novel *thoughts*! So, when you're curious about something, you release dopamine and thus become more motivated and action-oriented to learn new information and make new connections.[3] So get curious!

2. Pleasure and Pain

Neuroplasticity is heavily influenced by pain and pleasure. Things that we find fun and exciting, or threatening and harmful, are more readily encoded because they affect our survival. In this way the brain can easily reference pleasure as something to pursue, or something to avoid.

When we have a negative or fearful experience, for example, new connections "wire" faster in the brain. Things that might harm us, after all, are things we need front and center. Conversely, this neuroplasticity mechanism wires fast your fun and exciting experiences—even things that seem a little scary!

3. Purpose—Your "Why"

Dopamine is involved in more than just novelty. Dreams and goals have a powerful effect on the brain too. With the promise of a future reward, dopamine travels from the *nucleus accumbens* in our ancient brain to the decision-making area of our frontal lobe.

When it gets there, your level of consciousness increases,[4] and the promise of a future reward creates a critical ingredient for changing your life: *motivation*. This gives your brain a sense of purpose and direction, in the form of goals, dreams, and aspirations, and helps to keep your neuroplasticity switch on.

We've all had a lack of motivation from time to time, and for many of us, there have been good reasons why we temporarily lost our mojo. But one of those reasons is not because you were too lazy; so please don't label yourself that way. Instead, remember that your motivation can be stymied by boredom. And it can be stimulated by exploring new things. Just look for what excites you. Have fun! Innercises can help you tap into your motivation, into your decision-making circuits, and into your innate neuroplasticity.

4. Focus

Sure, it's great to expose yourself to a lot of new things and big dreams, but there are limits to a shotgun approach just as there are limits to chasing one shiny object after another. Enter focus. Innercises can help strengthen your ability to *focus* on your visions, goals, and needed actions. From professional violin players to Tibetan monks, those who diligently focus their attention on specific tasks show meaningful and measurable changes in their brains.[5] Research shows that mindfulness meditation in particular increases your ability to focus and remain optimistic. Mindful focusing is also linked to decreased activity in the fear and anxiety-based circuitry of the brain.[6]

By strengthening your "focus muscle," through learning to gradually increase your ability to narrow and sustain your attention, your neuroplasticity mechanisms can be trained to stay in the on position as your new normal.

5. Exercise

You could consider exercise to be the most critical Innercise of all. In general, *what's good for your body is good for your brain.* Exercise works its wonders in many ways, but a few key ones include

- Exercise feeds the brain. When you exercise, particularly aerobically, you increase blood and oxygen flow, and that means more support for the brain to work its magic.

- Exercise helps the brain create more connections by increasing neural growth factors.

- Exercise reduces stress and depression, and that can lead to more healthy brain cell growth.[7]

6. Discomfort

Your comfort zone is a space where your thoughts, feelings, and behaviors are most habitual. Where your brain runs its patterns on autopilot. The gorilla is napping and the orchestra is in tune. This is how most of us live our lives.

But when you're operating in this way, you're only creating a minimal number of new connections in your brain—after all, why bother if you don't need to when your existing ones are already doing the trick.

Stepping outside your comfort zone is similar to exploring novelties in that it exposes you to learning. When done deliberately though, you can stretch your mind even more. For example, casually meeting new people is a step. But what about making a presentation to a group of strangers? That sounds like a leap.

Neuroplasticity Is Always at Work

Take a moment now and count how many of the following statements are true for you:

- I meet new people every week.
- I engage in intense meaningful conversations every day.
- I'm physically active every single day.
- I deliberately engage in a variety of different projects each week.
- I have clear goals that I enjoy pursuing.
- I manage my stress levels.
- I focus intently on one task at a time.
- I take time to reflect on the meaning, purpose, and value of my life.
- I think about and emotionalize my goals and desires each day.
- I learn at least one significant new thing—a sport, a hobby, a skill—a year.
- I have a rich social life.
- I choose to constantly improve my health and diet.
- I like to try new experiences.
- I consciously pursue pleasurable activities every day.
- I challenge my old beliefs and seek new perspectives about other people, the world, and myself.

- I spend a few minutes every day in contemplative self-reflection.

- I spend a few minutes every day doing a spiritual practice (prayer, meditation, mindfulness, etc.).

- I read new and challenging books (fiction and nonfiction).

- I brainstorm with my friends and colleagues to find better ways to work and play.

- I seek to discover new levels of trust and intimacy with friends, partners, and family members.

- I practice being open-minded and accepting toward those who hold different beliefs.

- I look every day for ways to reinforce and create new empowering habits.

What's your score? Clearly, *more is better.*

Neuroplasticity is an ongoing process, and if you are committed to being the best person you can be, then it's a lifelong process.

Are You Ready for an Upgrade?

Our parents, teachers, siblings, and friends start us off in life. Those relationships, and the experiences in our young lives, condition us. They teach us our mindset, our skills, and our beliefs. And while much of this was vital at that time, and perhaps is still empowering in ways, a significant amount of it does not serve us well now as adults.

For example, there are likely times when you strive to achieve more, but lack the real tools required to make meaningful progress. In part that's because today's rules are constantly changing. But you don't have much control over this. Our brain's "software," with its ancient safety-conscious, energy-efficient, negatively oriented, change-hating propensity is another big part. But you do have considerable control over this.

In a manner of speaking, there are always new upgrades available to you:

- What if instead of running Fear 2.0, you could upgrade to Prosperity 6.1?

- What if instead of Anxiety 4.5, you could switch to Calmness X?

- What if instead of Broke version 1.16 you could download Wealth Premium? What about Energy Tracker? Or Happiness Pro?

Instead of operating at a low level of creativity and productivity—the thermostatic comfort zone of a habitualized brain where very little energy is spent on changing *anything* in your life—why not have the best brain you can? Why not? Seriously. Why not?

Neuroplasticity, combined with the newest discoveries in behavioral psychology is a game changer. It offers you the potential to literally change your brain and, as a result, your life. In the next chapter, I'll show you the easiest, fastest way to accomplish this.

Real People. Real Results.

Kay was an employee living paycheck to paycheck and earning $60,000 per year. Her bank account was often overdrawn and she constantly felt stressed and uncomfortable about being behind and playing catch up month after month. Not only that, but, as a single mom, not earning what she knew she was capable of earning meant she couldn't do many of the fun things she wanted to do with her daughter.

Kay says, "I've always been entrepreneurial, and I knew the level of time and financial freedom I've always wanted would not come working for someone else. I knew I was born to lead. I had goals, and a great work ethic, I but didn't know how to get there."

Kay has always felt grateful; however, she couldn't escape the fear that something could happen to her and the only source of income she had. She was scared that she would never get out of the cycle of barely earning enough and the thought of not reaching her financial and life goals were too much to bear. She constantly thought, "even though I've achieved some great things, why was I still on this financial hamster wheel? Would I ever truly achieve the financial breakthrough that I had been working on and taking action toward for so long?"

After discovering MyNeuroGym.com, in Kay's words, "I FINALLY HAVE FREEDOM!"

Kay is now successfully running her own coaching and training business and her lifestyle has changed dramatically. She is able to travel and show her daughter the power of setting and achieving goals firsthand. She says, "I am finally making the impact on my clients and the world that I know I'm meant to. I now have razor sharp focus on my goals and a clear and decisive plan of action to get there. There have been times when I literally could see my brain creating the plan of action for me to achieve goals I've had for years. I no longer have dread, overwhelm, or fear regarding my finances. I am relieved that I am now living the life of my dreams and I see more of it manifest each day. I thank God for this program. It is everything that I've needed and I'm overflowing with gratitude to John and the entire NeuroGym team."

Chapter Summary and Resources

Summary

Every time you think, feel, act, emotionalize, or remember, you reinforce existing brain neural connections or create new ones.

- Your brain is far more flexible than previously believed. It changes throughout your life using the innate mechanisms of neuroplasticity, with your willingness or without it.

- You can encourage neuroplasticity through curiosity, purpose, focus, exercise, fun, spaced repetition, and stepping out of your comfort zone.

Additional Free Resources

If you want additional help and free resources on how to best use each section in the book, I'm including some special coaching videos and 9 mini brain-training audios to go along with the book. I will act as your mindset coach as part of buying Innercise. For now, get started with this book and the free resources. Just scan the code below on your smartphone and log in to the NeuroGym platform or go to www.myneurogym.com/innercise to create a log in so you gain access to the free bonuses and resources.

Buff Your Brain

Using Innercise to Flex Your
Three Core Neuro-Muscles

"Biology gives you a brain. Life turns it into a mind."

—Jeffrey Eugenides, author

The message of neuroplasticity is that the *brain can be changed*. You can modify your old patterns, beliefs, and habits that keep you from achieving your goals.

But how do you change patterns? How do you, in essence, tinker with 100 billion brain cells and more than 100 trillion existing connections? I can show you with this little experiment:

Lift your hand up and look at your palm.

This simple act of lifting your hand is actually incredibly complex. It involves hormones and cells and nerves and electrochemical signals. Blood flow and oxygenation. Tendons and ligaments, muscles and bones. And it's almost entirely subconscious. Yet, you can do it with ease.

What's more, each time you do it, you *flex your bicep muscle.* Do it enough times, or add weights to give resistance, and your bicep will *strengthen.* You don't need to fully understand how this all works. When it comes to exercise, really you just need to *show up and do it.* Then commit to repeatedly showing and doing it to make your muscular and cardiovascular systems stronger. Innercising is much the same: You work out different "neuro-systems"—different neural "muscles" and "circuits"—and over time they become stronger.

Many physical exercise programs plan around working out certain muscles in particular groups—for example, arms, legs, and core—so that you can achieve specific strengthening. The same with aerobic exercise programs with plans to increase heart rate, burn fat, and improve oxygen flow.

Similarly, the Innercise program is planned toward measurable progress in reaching and then maintaining brain fitness. It's a plan that makes the most difference, gets the biggest results, and goes the furthest in aligning your conscious and subconscious processes. In particular, one that zeroes in on three main areas: *Awareness, Intention,* and *Action.*

After we introduce these three critical processes, I'll introduce you to the second foundational Innercise, "AiA." (Pronounced EYE-YA.)

WHAT ARE YOUR NEURO-MUSCLES?

Below are a few of the main components of brain fitness that are most critical to your success.

Your Three Core Neuro-Muscles

Awareness—We use this term most often to mean self-awareness—your ability to monitor your own mental, emotional, and physical state. Awareness is critical because it allows you to observe your habitual patterns and make changes.

Intention—This term refers to deciding how you want to think, feel, and act. When you begin to realize that your thoughts, feelings, and actions can be choices you make, you can choose more of what you want, and also more of what you don't want.

Action—This term is all about executing new ways of thinking, feeling, and behaving. Taking healthy, consistent constructive action is one of the best ways to build your brain fitness. When you take the right actions in the right order at the right time, you certainly increase your chances for success. But whether you succeed or fail, the action will strengthen your brain by learning—that strengthening is not a matter of chance but rather one of certainty.

Other Important Neuro-Muscle Considerations

Beliefs—Your ability to change the deeply rooted ideas and "truths" you hold about yourself and the world.

Habits—Your skill to identify and change automatic thoughts, emotions, and behaviors.

Focus—Your ability to narrow your attention to the task at hand.

Concentration—Your ability to sustain your focus.

Persistence—Your skill to pursue your goals, even when you're faced with challenges.

Resilience—Your ability to bounce back from adversity.

Resolve—Your ability to make firm decisions that lead to constructive action.

Creativity—Your ability to connect diverse concepts to generate new and useful ideas.

Visualization—Your ability to "see" something in detail in your mind's eye.

Confidence—Your ability to believe in yourself and the task at hand.

Willpower—Your capacity for self-control, especially when it comes to delaying gratification.

Attitude—Your ability to choose a positive mindset.

Gratitude—Your ability to appreciate what you have and what the painful lessons in your life can offer you.

Self-Talk—Your capacity to control and direct the "voice in your head."

Motivation—Your ability to push toward achieving your goals.

Maybe you are used to thinking of these as ordinary traits, ones you're born with or not. But the fact is you can improve and strengthen each of them when you commit to doing so.

NEURO-MUSCLE #1: AWARENESS

Think of the last time you said something you regretted. Perhaps you spoke in anger to a family member. Maybe you said something unkind to a friend.

First, cut yourself some slack. At least a little. We've all done this. It's a normal part of being human, and there's a good chance that what you said slipped out before you had a chance to catch yourself. Actually, now that you have some insight into how the brain works, you know the reason behind your slip-up: *your subconscious brain was in charge.* For example:

- You may have fallen back on an old habit of being sarcastic or negative when you felt jealous or judged.

- Or perhaps you tended to lash out verbally when you got stressed.

- Or maybe you felt the need to criticize others to cover your own lack of confidence in yourself.

Regardless, as soon as you felt uncomfortable—jealous, angry, hurt, threatened—your subconscious brain reacted with an automatic program to help relieve the tension. Out of your mouth came something that served to ease your discomfort, even if only briefly. But that quick fix usually comes with long-term consequences as you later may feel guilty, embarrassed, or ashamed: *I need to think before I open my mouth. I hurt the relationship and now I need to apologize to them. I need to earn back their trust.*

What if you could be more thoughtful in general—before you spoke, before you reacted, before you became impulsive?

For instance, catch yourself before you give in to eating that 600-calorie Danish cinnamon pastry that you swore off, or before you "Buy Now" another trinket on Etsy when you know you've got enough handcrafted accessories to fill a store. What if you could catch bad habits before they automatically run their course?

Well, it no longer has to be What if?

You can learn, first, to become aware of the trigger that sent you into your subconscious automatic reactions, and second, to become calm and consciously respond.

Why Awareness Matters

Awareness is the mental ability to *observe your thoughts, emotions, and behaviors without judgment*. It allows us to *catch the gorilla at work*. That's particularly important because we tend to only notice the gorilla after the deed is done—cigarette butts in the ashtray; five more pounds showing on the bathroom scale; the credit card bill we can't afford to pay. By observing ourselves in the moment, with practice, we can learn to interrupt negative or disempowering patterns, to stop them in their tracks, and instead fast track our conscious thoughts, feelings, and actions.

Your Brain on Awareness

We've learned a lot in recent years by studying people who invest a great deal of time practicing inner and outer awareness, and as a result have well-developed, self-observation skills. For example, monks, nuns, yogis, Sufis, and other contemplative practitioners, including millions of everyday people around the world—perhaps even yourself—who enjoy the virtues of what is now popularly known as mindfulness.[8]

What researchers have learned from studying these individuals is that *meditation, mindfulness, and self-reflection can dramatically change the brain, especially in the areas of the prefrontal cortex, and the insula and anterior cingulate. Importantly too, in the parietal lobe*—the part of your brain that gives you a sense of yourself and your relationship to others in the world.[9]

Please try this little demonstration now. Place your hand on your forehead, as if you are wiping your brow. Your prefrontal cortex is right behind your forehead. It's one of the newer areas of the brain in terms of evolution, and it's where you plan, make decisions, and regulate your behavior. It's the home of willpower, self-control, and imagination, and it's also one of areas that is stimulated by flexing your awareness muscle.

The insula and anterior cingulate are deeper structures found right behind your frontal lobes. They are part of your social brain and are more developed in primates, dolphins, whales, and humans than in any other species. These brain structures are essential for processing emotions like empathy, fairness, and self-love. Practicing self-awareness appears to be the most powerful and simplest way to strengthen this important part of your brain.

The Magic of Awareness: Choice

Awareness is perhaps the most important mental function that can change the brain. If a magic genie appeared and granted you only one wish for your brain fitness, go with *to increase awareness.*

The reason? Without awareness, you won't even know if your brain is or isn't working well. So, the moment you become aware of your thoughts, feelings, habits, and behaviors you can assess—then keep what works and change what doesn't. You have that *choice.* When you observe yourself in the moment—when you see your mental, emotional, and behavioral patterns *as they begin,* you increase your ability to control negative conditioning and proclivities. You can choose good habits. You can choose to remain calm. You can choose to take constructive action. And every time you make these healthy choices, your neuroplasticity—and possibilities—increase.

NEURO-MUSCLE #2: INTENTION

Choice is the magic ingredient in the recipe for the life you want. As you build awareness, you build choices. And as you build choices, you build the power of *intention.*

Intention refers to *deciding how you want to think, feel, and act.*

Like awareness, intention is part of the neural circuitry that activates the prefrontal cortex, the home of your inner genius. Intention opens up a whole new world for you through self-reflective questions such as

•   What do I think, feel, or do now?

- What is the goal here?
- What is truly important to me?

NEURO-MUSCLE #3: ACTION

Alan Brown, my mentor who helped me understand the distinction between being interested and being committed, was also the first person to teach me that deciding what you want was only the first step on the journey to getting what you want.

After that lunch together some thirty years ago, Alan began to teach me the techniques he had used to become successful. He had me start by writing out my goals. Financial goals, life goals—whatever it was that I wanted, he made me write it out, by hand, in detail. In essence, he guided me toward *deciding on my intentions for my life.*

I was cool with all of this. At nineteen, I was cool with most anything just like every other kid who thought he was invincible, which turned out to be most of the kids I hung out with back in the day. But then things got weird.

He told me I had to read my goals every day. *Fair enough*, I thought. But then he said I had to run my fingers over them. To visualize and feel them as if they were really happening. To see myself in vivid detail actually achieving them.

This is crazy, I said to myself. *I'm not comfortable with this. What a waste of time.* But whenever I heard this in my head, I would think back to that big question he'd asked me over lunch: "Are you interested, or are you committed?"

Yeah, I was committed and so I did what he told me. Every day for *two years,* I dedicated the time to follow all of his instructions. *I took action daily* based on what I needed to do. I focused on my goals. I taped them to my bathroom mirror and looked at it daily as I brushed my teeth and took care of my other bathroom related business. I read those goals regularly. I moved my fingers over them. I wrote and rewrote them. And, more than anything else, I visualized them in exhaustive detail.

You have to remember I was nineteen then, and despite whatever might have been going on inside me, outwardly I usually projected myself as already knowing how to change the world. Being humble was not in my wheelhouse. So, you can imagine my surprise when I began to notice a host of problems I was dealing with begin to decrease, and then to dissolve altogether—things like my desire to shut up the noise in my head about failing or looking like a fool in front of my friends and family. Even when those negative thoughts began to emerge, I discovered that my ability to refocus on my goals and the task at hand made the voices fade away.

In my first year, following what Alan taught me, I earned $30,000 selling real estate in Toronto. For a nineteen-year-old in the early '80s, this was real money. I was making more than anyone my age, at least those I knew of, and plenty more than a lot of grown-up realtors working out of the same office as me. In my second year I hit $151,000. Fears of ending up like my dad were by now a distant memory, an impossibility, and in fact my life continued to become more like what I had envisioned.

What Alan did was teach me to take action, beginning with learning to focus *on my intentions* and that matters for two reasons. The first is that *anything important you want to accomplish in life requires sustained focus.* You can't expect to lose weight and keep it off, or build great relationships, or start a successful business, or make any other significant life changes that will stick unless you have a focused effort over time. The crash diet, the quick fix, the weekend seminar—they're just bursts of short-lived energy. They're only sprints, while reaching your goals requires the mental fitness of a marathoner. You need sustained action to succeed.

The second reason that taking focused action matters is that creating new brain pathways for thinking, feeling, and behaving requires time and repetition. So, you're going to need to Innercise regularly to get the results you want.

Many years later after Alan told me to run my fingers over my goals, we now know that visualizing is in itself an action that literally can change the brain.[10] For example, research shows that just *imagining* playing a sequence of piano notes can create changes in the parts of the brain you'd find if you *actually physically* played the sequence on a piano. That study and others like it are some of the greatest examples of how you can truly change the brain through mental and emotional effort.[11]

Mindfulness Bell: Focus, Calm, and Awareness

Many people find meditation challenging. Even the Dalai Lama admits that he sometimes has trouble settling down to meditate. I think then that you will find this Innercise helpful to get you started. It's based simply on *listening to a sound.*

You can do this using a mindfulness bell—that's one with a resonant tone that gradually diminishes. You can also use a regular bell. Or, to be really easy about it, simply download one of the many mindfulness bell apps onto your computer or use your smartphone.

Set the bell to go off once or twice an hour. When you hear the bell, just pause for a few moments and try one of the following Innercises:

Brief: When you hear the bell, just listen to it with full awareness and attentiveness as it fades into silence.

Moderate: Ring the bell and listen with greater attentiveness, as if you've never heard a bell in your life. What does it really sound like? How does it affect your thoughts, your mood, and your body?

Intense: Ring the bell and listen as the sound resonates and then begins to diminish. As it fades, listen as closely as you can, with as much intensity as you can muster. When it fades altogether, listen to the sounds in the room and then to the sounds of your own breathing for an additional 60 seconds. Then quietly observe how your thoughts and feelings have changed. Finally, focus on what you intend to do for the next hour.

INNERCISE: AiA ("Eye-Ya")

Let me introduce you to another keystone Innercise you can use every day to gain more self-control and awareness. This Innercise flexes all three of your core neuro-muscles. It's called *AiA* (pronounced "eye-ya") and stands for

A: Awareness
I: Intention
A: Action

Whenever you are feeling stressed, anxious, worried, unhappy, resentful, angry, or disappointed with any result or situation, pause and first do the Innercise we talked about before: "Take Six."

"TAKE 6: Calm the Circuits"

Take six deep rhythmic breaths in through your nose and out through your mouth, like you are blowing out of a straw. As you breathe in, say,

I breathe in calmness, I breathe out stress.
or
I breathe in calmness, I breathe out fear.
or
I breathe in calmness, I breathe out anxiety, or overwhelm.

Next, do this AiA Innercise:

In a calm relaxed frame of mind (as you gently breathe in and out) be aware of your physiology, your mental and emotional state, and the behavior you are engaged in. (Awareness)

Next ask yourself "What is my intention for this moment?" Is it to be angry? Sad? Mad or frustrated, or to be calm and respond instead of react? (Intention)

Once you choose your intention, take one small, simple action-step toward achieving your goal. (Action)

Learning this process teaches you to be in awareness and moves you out of an automatic reactive state and into a pro-active state that you have more control over. With practice it can become the new default pattern that serves you well.

. . . .

How the Three Foundational Neuro-Muscles Work Together

Now, reflect back again on the last time you said something you wished you hadn't. Now imagine how that interaction could have changed if you had applied the following three principles:

First, by taking a slow, gentle breath and increasing your *awareness*, you could have noticed that you were upset.

Second, that new awareness could have given you the freedom to create an *intention* of how you would have liked that interaction to go. Would you want to say something you would regret, or would you want to take the higher road?

Third, with this deeper understanding you could take *action* to move closer to your intention. How could you best serve the other person? What could you say or do that could make the relationship stronger?

Together, these three neuro-muscles form a powerful combination, one you can use for deep, extended periods of time, but also in lightning quick moments. They're a winning combination for achieving your goals.

But as you no doubt know, any change has more than its fair share of obstacles. In the next section of this book, we'll look at the five main obstacles to change, and how you can use Innercise to shift each of them to help you reach your highest potential.

Real People. Real Results.

Alisha felt overworked and underappreciated while working 50 plus hours per week as an associate chiropractor in someone else's veterinary business. For many years she tried to launch her own side business but found herself exhausted and burned out after working 50 plus hours week after week. She didn't have the energy to go out with friends or family and felt like she was missing out on life. The pressure to do a good job and get a steady paycheck was almost unbearable. In addition, Alisha recalls, "I had a lot of fear and worry that I was not good enough. I was afraid of receiving love due to not feeling adequate and from being hurt in the past. I had just broken up with my boyfriend and I knew I wanted more out of life but was not sure how to get it."

Alisha came across a free MyNeuroGym.com webinar and decided to check it out. Then she decided to start one of the offered brain training programs. She diligently watched the training videos and listened daily to the powerful Innercises. She says, "Something happened that I never anticipated. My thoughts started to change. I started connecting with a deeper strength and intuition, and I started believing in myself."

Alisha was soon faced with a difficult decision at her job. She was told that she was not working hard enough, and she needed to do more. She says, "This previously would have destroyed me as my work ethic is extremely important to me. However, a funny thing happened. I didn't take it personally at all! The numbers showed that I was outperforming every other employee and I knew if I could do this for someone else, I could definitely do it for myself." Right then, she decided to take a leap of faith, leave her associate job, and put her trust in herself and in growing her part-time business.

In a matter of weeks, her part-time business doubled, and she was able to support herself. "I felt a huge burden lifted and my soul felt so alive. I was able to rest and rejuvenate my body and my mind. I was meeting friends for coffee and going on hikes, doing all the things I had wanted to do. I felt like I had been in jail and now was free. THIS was what I wanted for my life. I just needed to be brave enough to see it." With her newfound confidence, strength, and some extra time on her hands, she was able to "fuel her soul!" In addition, within the first year Alisha was able to pay off over $50,000 in debt. Something she had wanted to do for a very long time.

"Thank goodness I decided to check this program out because it changed my life. It gave me true wealth and abundance. I found that wealth is not just about the money, it's about a wealthy life: great relationships, health, happiness, and joy. This program gave me the tools to be truly rich."

Chapter Summary and Resources

Summary

- Just as exercise can strengthen your physical muscles, Innercise can strengthen your "neuro-muscles."

- There are three core neuro-muscles:

  - *Awareness*, to bring new insight to things inside and outside you that you barely notice and to give you the ability to *choose*.

  - *Intention*, to use the choice offered by awareness to *decide what it is that you want*.

  - *Action*, to focus on that chosen path and deliberately choose how you will think, feel, and act.

- These core neuro-muscles are most effective when repeatedly combined over extended periods of time.

- Innercises are fast, reliable techniques to help you strengthen each of your core neuro-muscles.

Additional Free Resources

If you want additional help and free resources on how to best use each section in the book, I'm including some special coaching videos and 9 mini brain-training audios to go along with the book. I will act as your mindset coach as part of buying Innercise. For now, get started with this book and the free resources. Just scan the code below on your smartphone and log in to the NeuroGym platform or go to www.myneurogym.com/innercise to create a log in so you gain access to the free bonuses and resources.

PART II:

Master Your Thoughts and Emotions

"What stands in the way becomes the way."

—Marcus Aurelius

Gorilla Warfare

The Five Shifts of Innercise

"Nothing is an obstacle unless you say it is."

—Wally Amos

A ton of people achieve their goals pretty regularly—in fact, you've probably already achieved many goals in your own life. But when you try to tackle the more important ones—the ones that stretch you the most, the ones with more change at stake—the more your subconscious mind, your gorilla, will want to keep you stuck under the guise that this is where you are safest.

The gorilla has a number of tricks to keep you the way you are. The chapters that follow will help you understand those tricks, these obstacles, and then how to use *Innercise* to move beyond them.

What Do You Think You Need to Do to Reach Your Goals?

To understand more precisely how the gorilla is keeping you stuck, we need to look at how you've been taught to get what you want in life.

Basically, the story is about the same for most of us. Our parents, teachers, colleagues, bosses, and just about everyone else tell us: If you set your mind to something and work hard enough at it, you'll win.

- *Want to earn more?* Set a goal for your income, work hard at your job or business, and *bingo!* there it is.

- *Want to lose weight?* Set a target for your new weight, eat less, exercise more, and *voilà.*

- *Want to start a business?* Envision your dream biz, then go build it, and *tah-dah!*

Or maybe you can relate to this better as a visual:

Chances are you already smell a rat. Maybe you've abandoned this fantasy or maybe you are still holding on to it. I mean, we all want to believe there is justice and fairness in life. That the pure of heart and mind combined with a strong effort makes all that is right in the world. Unfortunately, that's not the way it is. If it was, life would be easy.

We'd all be rich, happy, and healthy.

The truth is, setting goals is the simple part. Taking the necessary action and following through, persevering even when things look bleak, and being consistent about it is when you come to see that the answers you seek are already within you.

This brings up a common problem for most people when it comes to change. We think we need to know more, but knowledge is rarely the problem. We've got enough "how-to" already. We know how to be at peace, for example, but the actual process to get there is quite a lot more involved. That's why, despite all our knowledge,

- 95 percent or more of dieters regain all the weight they lost.
- 80 percent of new businesses fail within five years.
- 40 percent of the marriages of young couples fail within five years.
- Over 70 percent of lottery winners lose their money within three years.

The real issue is that we are generally unable to consistently stick with the behaviors that can help us be successful. What happens then is we usually end up getting the same old results. Worse still, instead of acknowledging that the old ways aren't working, we often tell ourselves, *I just didn't try hard enough, or the timing was bad, or it wasn't my fault...* and repeat the cycle again. I share your frustration. I repeat cycles too. But not as much and with far fewer consequences thanks to Innercise.

What ACTUALLY Happens When You Try to Reach Your Goals

The Goal-Behavior-Results fantasy doesn't take into account enough about what goes on in your subconscious mind.

But the gorilla does, and it's got its hands in *everything*. Everything has to pass through your subconscious to make sure it doesn't rock your comfort zone.

In effect, you need the gorilla's approval to make things happen. And that's tough to get when your conscious and subconscious processes aren't aligned. For example,

- You might set a goal to increase your income, but when it comes to taking the necessary action, like making sales calls, asking for a raise, or networking, somehow more "important" things always seems to come up, so you do those instead of what's really important to you.

- You might decide to lose weight, but when your alarm goes off an hour earlier to allow time for a walk, you press "snooze" once, twice, three times, four times, until you fall back into your routine of making a mad dash to get out the door so you're not late for work, school, or whatever compels you to get out of bed now.

It can seem as if your ambition is fed into a black box that turns it into "No thanks, I'm good with where I'm at."

Gorilla Warfare: The 6 Brain Obstacles to Success

What exactly is going on in that black box of your subconscious brain? How is it that the gorilla keeps you stuck? In Innercise, we identify **six main obstacles to success**: fear, excess stress, limiting beliefs, negative mindset, lack of emotional control, and disempowering habits. We'll discuss each in detail in the following five chapters and provide you with Innercises to help overcome them. For now, though, here's a brief overview of each:

Obstacle 1: Fear

The primary concern of your brain is to keep you alive and safe, and it has developed a very sensitive system, starring, among other things, a brain structure called the *amygdala*. Right now, at this very minute, that system is alert and ready, evaluating every perception as friend or foe.

This system is operating without your awareness, and for most of us, it rings an alarm bell every time it senses a foe. It even reacts to your worrisome thoughts as if they were real, external threats. For example, this crosses everyone's mind when they board an airplane: "What if we crash?" And if you have a fear of flying, it can be more than just a passing thought; it can be emotionally paralyzing. Either way, your alarm system flashes warning lights about this "foe." Statistically speaking, though, the chances of being in a plane crash are an astonishing 1 in 11 million. One in 11 million! You want to know what is more likely? Dating a supermodel (1 in 88,000) or becoming a movie star (1 in 1.5 million)—these are definitely "friends," but your system is likely to pass over these more pleasurable odds and stay ready at the helm to sound off alarms about the greatest improbabilities.

Whenever those bells go off, and they do regularly, the gorilla will find a way to bring you back to its perception of safety. If you see a real snake, you'll feel the sensation of a dozen stress neurochemicals rushing through your body. The same is true when simply imagine one slithering close by; you'll feel a similar sensation from the dozens of stress neurochemicals that are released. Or, you could have plenty of money in the bank, but a historically predictable correction in the stock market can leave you feeling like poverty is on your doorstep.

These real or imaginary fears can cripple your optimism and desire to take action or improve. For example, you might stay in a stifling job just making ends meet rather than searching for employment that will pay you more for your talents and raise your standard of living. You might look away when an interesting person enters your space for fear of being rejected instead of being emotionally available and meeting that special someone you yearn for. And even if you *do* start to make progress toward achieving your goals, it's likely you'll sabotage yourself with chronic, impulsive, automatically triggered worries. According to Dr. Srini Pillay, there are more than twenty-five different types of fears that can derail you, if not completely stop you dead in your tracks. You can learn to recognize these obstacles when they show up and turn them into fuel for your success.

Obstacle 2: Limiting Beliefs and Stories

Beliefs are the lenses through which you interpret the world and your experiences, and they color everything you say, think, and do. But beliefs are simply reinforced patterns in your brain, and they are mostly based on memories, personal experiences, and old models of reality.

Here's an example of when beliefs run head-on into a counter-belief. Lottery winners are more likely to declare bankruptcy within three to five years than the average American, and about 70 percent of all lottery winners, as well as those who gain a large windfall, end up bankrupt. On top of that, many of these "lucky" people say winning was one of the worst things that ever happened to them. Instead of getting them out of financial trouble, it got them into it. What?! A $300 million winning ticket?! When the infamous Jack Whittaker, already a millionaire, won that $300 million and then went broke, he was asked if life was easier before the lottery jackpot, and he said, "Yeah, it was a lot easier then."

But why? The answer is that there's disconnect between these lottery winners' subconscious self-image and sense of self-worth—what they believe to be true about themselves—and what they are now challenged to believe about themselves with their newfound wealth. Their outside environment doesn't match their internal map of their sense of self-worth. When that happens, most do anything, and most of it unconsciously, to essentially self-sabotage to bring things back into alignment. Back to the way things were. This is a perfect example of cognitive dissonance in full force.

Limiting beliefs can cause you to act habitually, and often interfere with your ability to see yourself, other people, and the world in new, more empowering ways. So, until you change those limiting beliefs, you'll keep repeating the same patterns that hold you back.

Obstacle 3: A Negative Mindset

We all go through periods of being negative or pessimistic. It's just a part of your brain's warning system to make sure you look for danger before leaping into action. From an evolutionary perspective, being skeptical, unsure, and negative is a valuable trait. It helps stop you from impulsively indulging in risky behavior, like gambling or overeating. It tells you to take extra caution when spending money or committing to a relationship with someone you barely know. Not so incidentally, those lottery winners who lose it all—well, they stop listening to their warning systems, think self-discipline no longer applies, and indulge in throwing around money like there's no tomorrow.

On the other hand, if you start to *ruminate* on all the possible negative things that could happen, your fear and anxiety circuits can take control of your brain, turning you from the optimist that is the natural mindset of a healthy brain into an entrenched pessimist where unnatural negativity reigns. And too much of this negativity can generate excess stress, which further deepens the disruption of a healthy functioning brain. In short, negativity has its benefits when looking at the balanced whole picture where positivity and happiness are even more beneficial powerful forces.

Obstacle 4: Excess Stress

Whenever you feel worried, anxious, afraid, or exhausted, your brain sends out a stress response by way of neurochemicals. The result can be havoc. Stress can interfere with your ability to learn new skills; turn off your motivation center in your brain; keep your body in a constant state of unrest; interfere with your sleep; and cloud your brain's executive functioning.

Stress can also inhibit the most creative parts of your brain, leaving you less able to see new opportunities, to generate creative ideas, and to access your inner genius. But like negativity, it's not all or nothing: a healthy amount of stress keeps you alert, excited, and motivated.

Obstacle 5: Disempowering Habits

There's an old saying I'll paraphrase here: We become what we feel and what we do. Day after day, over the course of years, those autopilot patterns in our brains—we can just call them habits—come to define us. Scientists studying behavior and the brain know that our habits are extremely "sticky"—they become very easy to repeat and very difficult to change.

Part of this is from our wiring. As I wrote earlier, the brain loves to create habits so it can save energy; it's a lot easier to automatically carry out familiar tasks without thinking about them than it is to innovate. Sure, it can go both ways. If you're in the habit of exercising five times a week, good on you. If you're in the habit of setting aside 10 percent of your monthly income for savings, that's great. If you're in the habit of carrying on a family tradition of Sunday night dinner with no TV and no smartphones, that too is wonderful. Those habits can be empowering. They can elevate you.

The wrong habits though—many of which had their seeds planted in your childhood—are largely destructive and disempowering. They can stop you from seeing new solutions to a better quality of life. They can cause cognitive bias blinding us from a more truthful worldview. For example, "I've been having bacon and eggs my whole life. So, what if I have high cholesterol, I don't care. I'll take Metformin. Besides, I've got good genes—my grandfather ate worse than I do and he lived to be ninety-eight." Or, "I'm just going to keep leveraging my assets using debt. If banks want to give me lines of credit, it's on them too. It's not like they don't want me to borrow. Of course, they do. They make boatloads off the interest I pay. So, it's good for them; it's good for me." Or, "You know all of this stuff about body image and fat shaming. Everybody's overweight. At least everyone I see. So, I'm not going to feel bad that I'm 20 or 25 pounds overweight. Skinny people are miserable anyway. If they let go and enjoyed life more, like me, they'd be a lot better off."

Obstacle 6: Lack of Emotional Control

Psychologist Dr. Joan Rosenberg, highly regarded for her expertise in emotional intelligence, taught me an amazing way to help reframe my ideas about emotions. She said that emotions are neither good nor bad, positive nor negative, regardless of whether they feel pleasant or unpleasant in varying degrees. Emotions are triggered at the subconscious level, which in turn triggers the neurochemistry that causes feelings we are aware of. Sure, we tend to move away from or suppress unpleasant feelings and move toward and try to accelerate pleasant ones. The key is to be more aware of our feelings without judgment and to learn how to deliberately and skillfully manage them better.

These six obstacles are lurking both above and below the surface of our consciousness. Until we learn to be more aware and more nonjudgmentally observant as the most effective path to finding solutions, we may very well reach some of our goals, but not our highest potential.

INNERCISE: Gratitude Tree

Note: Some Innercises, like this one, are best done with your eyes closed. In those cases, you'll want to read through the Innercise first to make sure you understand each step or visit www.myneurogym.com/innercise where you can find helpful audio/video versions to guide you through.

Close your eyes, take six deep breaths, and calm your circuits. Get into a totally relaxed, calm, peaceful state of mind and being.

As you do this, imagine that you are the trunk of a tree, without any branches or twigs or leaves. Now let's start building your gratitude tree.

Think of one thing you are extremely grateful for. It can be a person, your heartbeat, or your fingers. You can be grateful for being alive today. You can be grateful for being able to breathe, you can be grateful for having eyes that see, you can be grateful for having awakened spiritually. Think of whatever you are most grateful for in this moment.

Next, feel the love and appreciation for whatever you have chosen to be grateful about. As you inhale and exhale, choose to be aware of the emotions and sensations that being grateful bring to you.

When you choose to build your gratitude tree with the personal or professional things that you are grateful for, you are activating the neurochemistry of gratitude and appreciation.

The more you find to be grateful for, the more you train your brain to find even more to be grateful for. No matter how hard things are in your life, learning to be grateful for the complex and the simple is an amazing tool to use for refocusing your mind.

Cognitive Biases

In his excellent book *The Brain Revolution: Know and Train New Brain Habits*, Dr. Evian Gordon reveals a long list of ways in which our brain habits can lead us astray. Here are just a few of the ways you may be fooling yourself, without being aware of them:

- *Blind spot bias*—the tendency to see yourself as less biased than others

- *Confirmation bias*—the tendency to seek, interpret, and remember information in a way that confirms what you already believe

- *Attentional bias*—the tendency to pay attention to and remember emotional or novel stimuli

- *Bandwagon bias*—the tendency to do or believe things because many other people do

- *Streak bias and small number bias*—the tendency to see false patterns and order and causality that isn't there

- *Scarcity bias*—the tendency to see those things in limited supply as being more valuable

- *Payment bias*—the tendency to demand much more to give up an object than one would be willing to pay to acquire it

- *Consensus bias*—the tendency to overestimate how much other people agree with you

- *Loss aversion bias*—the tendency to react more strongly to losses than to gains

- *Negativity bias*—the tendency to magnify threat and have greater recall of unpleasant memories than positive ones

- *Positivity bias*—the tendency to be overly optimistic

To help discover which obstacles are holding you back the most, please visit www.myneurogym.com/innercise and complete a free assessment. It will help you identify limiting stories, beliefs, and habits that are keeping you stuck.

Aligning the Gorilla: The 5 Shifts of Innercise

Your subconscious is a permanent part of you. Period. So, you have to learn to live with it. The best way is to learn to align your subconscious more closely with what you truly want; to learn to transform your brain so that you view obstacles as opportunities for greater strength. You can, in effect, recruit the power of your subconscious brain—your gorilla—to help you reach your goals. For example,

Your fears can become fuel for change instead of holding you back.

Your beliefs can become powerful stories and anchors that inspire you instead of keeping you stuck in the status quo.

Your mindset can become a lens for seeing possibility and opportunity all around you instead of making you unhappy and cynical.

Your stress can become the most powerful tool for building your resilience and creativity instead of burning you out.

Your habits can become rituals that bring you steadily closer to your goals instead of steadily shrinking your life.

You might be saying to yourself now, *Okay great, but how do I do this?* The answer: with Innercise, a multifaceted tool—a Swiss Army knife for moving your life forward.

In the five chapters that follow, you'll learn to unearth this power already inside you, just waiting for you to tap into it.

Real People. Real Results.

Karen had been a realtor for thirty-one years at the time she first saw an invitation for the Brain-A-Thon, a free training hosted by NeuroGym. She usually ignored these types of invitations, but something about the Brain-A-Thon piqued her interest.

"I had no idea what I was in for that afternoon! All I knew was that I looked forward to it with excitement, grabbed a notebook, and cleared the space on my calendar. I was so fascinated by the content, I filled a whole notebook with notes and couldn't wait to hear what the next speaker had to share!

Her gamble paid off. "I threw myself into Innercising daily, not having any expectations other than blind faith and an open mind. A lot has happened in these last few months. And though it has been gradual, I feel a sense of freedom and release that was not there before. The biggest and best result was realizing how many emotional pains and self-limiting beliefs I had cursed myself with and how I now had the power to release them. When they try to creep back in I tell myself I am done with that. It does not serve my life. I am moving forward.

"I have already tripled my income these first six months of the year over my annual income for the past ten years. I know I am going to double that in the second half of the year. For me, as vital as the income is for my family (as my hardworking husband became disabled last year), the true gift is the freedom from the mental and emotional blockages that plagued me all my life."

Karen spent most of her career believing that she didn't have what it took to close bigger deals and approach the kind of clients who could lead to bigger commissions. But after she started Innercising she released all of these false beliefs, fears, and stories she kept telling herself. For her, it wasn't about skills or knowledge. It was about learning how to get her brain in alignment with what she knew she deserved.

Chapter Summary and Resources

Summary

- The old model of "set a goal, do the right things, and get the results" doesn't work.

- Living up to your highest potential is more than know-how. It's also about doing more of what you know you need to be doing.

- There are six common obstacles to successfully reaching your goals: *fear, limiting beliefs, a negative mindset, excess stress, and disempowering habits.*

Additional Free Resources

If you want additional help and free resources on how to best use each section in the book, I'm including some special coaching videos and 9 mini brain-training audios to go along with the book. I will act as your mindset coach as part of buying Innercise. For now, get started with this book and the free resources. Just scan the code below on your smartphone and log in to the NeuroGym platform or go to www.myneurogym.com/innercise to create a log in so you gain access to the free bonuses and resources.

Habits

From Autopilot to Conscious Control

"Plant a tiny seed in the right spot, and it will grow without coaxing."

—Dr. B. J. Fogg

A number of years ago my wife and I chartered a catamaran for a trip in French Polynesia from the private island of Vahine to Bora Bora. It was a five-hour voyage through the classical South Pacific paradise of so many movies and books, and the beauty of the sea and surrounding islands was breathtaking.

The enchantment was broken partway through the trip, however, when I was walking past a bridge on my way to the stern and noticed something unusual: no one at the helm. It was a little unsettling. There we were, plowing through three-foot waves in the Pacific Ocean, with no captain!

It turned out there was a simple explanation. The captain had entered the coordinates for Bora Bora into the onboard autopilot-sailing program, and *it* was staying the course, so he could do other things.

That autopilot at work on the catamaran is a great metaphor for much of what happens in your life all the time. The reinforced neural patterns in your brain are like autopilots staying the course for your life, steering you toward destinations, some paradises like Bora Bora, while others…no offense intended, more like North Korea.

Just as you have neural patterns for brushing your teeth with the same hand in the same way, you also have habits for how you think and even how you *feel*. In fact, it's not a stretch to say that from a neural perspective, your life is made up almost entirely of habits.

They allow your brain to get more stuff done. Like the captain of the catamaran, when you hand common tasks off to your autopilot—your subconscious brain—you've got more bandwidth left to do tasks that require added brainpower.

Habits work great *as long as they take you to where you want to go.* When they don't, they can stop you from working efficiently. They can cause frustration. They can make you procrastinate. They can turn off the motivation and creativity centers in your brain. They can disempower you. They can lead you to gain weight, get in over your head in debt, ruin relationships. And even kill you—on average, smokers die ten years sooner than nonsmokers.

How Habits Work: The Psychology

Habits form over time by repeating certain thoughts, feelings, or behaviors until they become firmly embedded as memories. Some can be instilled consciously, but more often they form without us even being aware of them. When we cruise on the freeway at 65 mph for ten miles and have little recognition of stepping on the accelerator or brakes, or changing lanes, it might seem like magic. But really, it's your subconscious mind guiding a complex collection of habits all bundled together.

To get inside the magic, behavioral psychologists have broken habits down into three specific parts: the *trigger*, the *behavior*, and the *reward*. This model gives us a way to not only better understand habits but also how to better create and reinforce empowering ones and change disempowering ones.

Using this three-part habit model, let's break down a common habit: the ritual of your morning coffee.

1. *The trigger:* Your alarm goes off and that starts the morning coffee sequence in your brain. Your coffee trigger could also be a person, a time of day, an emotional state, or any number of things.

2. *The behavior:* You walk to the kitchen and sip your coffee that's brewed and at the right temperature thanks to your automated coffee maker.

3. *The reward:* You feel the effects of the invigorating caffeine and the pleasurable dopamine released by your brain and tell yourself, Hey, do this again.

These three steps are called the *habit loop*. The more you run a loop, the more your brain gets used to doing it, and the more ingrained the neural patterns become.

Habits, in fact, are much like addictions. So breaking habit loops usually have headways and relapses, just as is true for kicking addictions. In a practical sense, it means manipulating one of the three steps in the process. But which one?

Unfortunately, the *reward* step—the dopamine release—is too late in the cycle. By the time you've reached that point, the cycle is already complete. You've had your coffee and you've strengthened the ingrained neural patterns a little more.

Simply *not* doing the *behavior*, as we all know, is equally challenging. Change, as we have discussed, is challenging on its own. But with habits, it's often even more challenging because the patterns are decidedly in your subconscious, sneaking around. When faced with the same triggers—for instance your alarm going off—resisting the urge to act on the habitual behavior—drinking your morning coffee—requires a never-ending supply of willpower. Research, and no doubt your personal experience, suggests this is no easy task.

Which brings us to *the triggers*. In fact, this is exactly where to start. Identify the *triggers* so you can disrupt and then ultimately break the cycle before the next two steps even show up. This is one reason why alcoholics may tend to stay away from stressful situations, or distance themselves from friends who drink. Stress and other drinkers are triggers. And while it's important to be able to recognize these two, avoidance is not usually a tidy cleanup. Alcoholics may be able to avoid stress and drinking buddies, but there could be a hundred different triggers. *No more golf because I'll want a cold beer once I'm back in the clubhouse. No more cola because it'll make me want my usual rum and Coke.* It's impossible for any of us to live in a bubble with no triggers, and in fact too much avoidance can lead to loneliness and other problems. The same is true with the coffee ritual: You can't avoid waking up. And the urge to have a clear and alert mind could just lead you to find another stimulant.

What the act of identifying the major triggers *does* do, however, is offer a neurological window into the habit system so that we can do what we really need to do: *Replace* unhealthy behaviors. We can use Innercise to both hack into the habit loop and then replace those behaviors. New behaviors will help desensitize other related triggers that can lead to our disempowerment.

Have you ever been obsessively upset, experienced a sudden change, and then later realized you'd "forgotten" what you were bothered about before?

What happened was you somehow interrupted the emotional and mental track you were on. Here are a few ways you can deliberately interrupt other disempowering habitual loops:

- Stand up, move around, walk, jump
- Sing
- Dance
- Clap your hands
- Laugh
- Listen to music
- Read

Anything that interrupts your pattern can help change your state—the right distraction can make all the difference!

. . . .

Innercise: Identifying Habits and Triggers

Because habits can be difficult to identify at first, you may want to repeat the following exercise for several days:

1. Identify your negative/unwanted/destructive habits

What are your top three daily negative/disempowering habits?

Which single habit, if you changed it, could have the biggest positive impact on your life?

2. Identify the trigger(s) for your habit

What happens *just before* you engage in your habit?

3. Find a replacement behavior

List three positive/empowering behaviors you could do in place of the negative/disempowering ones you usually do when triggered.

. . . .

Habitus Interruptus: Using Innercise to Change Habits

Several years ago, one of my best friends, Robert May, and I planned a trip to Las Vegas to celebrate my birthday. Our itinerary included a few nights at the Encore Hotel, a favorite of mine.

I was very much looking forward to the time away, but there was a catch. I had recently made a conscious decision to deal with a destructive habit that had plagued me for years: my addiction to sugar.

I loved desserts and sweet sauces. If it had sugar, it was for me. But then I began to notice my body was paying a price for my sweet tooth. My joints ached. My stomach hurt. I gained weight. And—if you don't already know this about me, then I'll just say I'm very motivated—I found myself throughout each day increasingly having to stop and restart with sugar hits to keep up my energy level. It had all reached a head earlier in the year, and I was determined to change.

So yes, Vegas would pose a problem. The restaurant in the Encore had one of the most spectacular dessert bars in the world. There were probably ten sections of their buffet devoted just to desserts. For a runaway sugar addict like I was, it was the Promised Land; heaven on earth; a shrine to all that is sweet. "This trip," I told Robert, "is going to push every sugar button I have." For all my conscious determination, I still knew I would be swimming against a riptide.

Fortunately, I also understood my habit loop, and how I could Innercise in advance.

Scientists at the Massachusetts Institute of Technology had discovered that you *can* use your awareness to alter any circuits that automatically drive behavior. Meaning, though habits are mostly at the subconscious level, your conscious brain still has some say about things.

My first step was to identify the main trigger. I knew just the sight of that buffet filled with delicious desserts would start my mouth salivating, my brain anticipating the sugar rush ahead, and if I didn't consciously interrupt the habit loop right then, I'd load up on pastries and treats, and scarf them down.

So, the sight of the dessert buffet—the main trigger—was my opportunity to use my *awareness muscle*, call on my conscious brain, and choose a different behavior.

I knew quite well too that this was easier to say than to do. We've all made promises about changing our habits, but when the triggers appear, we fall back on our old patterns, sometimes without even realizing it.

So, to beat my sugar habit, I needed to mentally *rehearse what it would be like to NOT allow the habit loop and the anticipation of the dopamine hit, to control me.* That's when I decided to use an Innercise called Mental Rehearsal.

First, I went online and downloaded a beautiful color image of the dessert bar. Then, I began to imagine I was there in the Encore. I pictured walking amongst the delicious desserts. To my left Crème Brûlée. To my right Tarte Tatin. In front of me, calling my name, my favorite, tiramisu with dark chocolate mousse. I breathed in the aroma. I heard the other diners. I imagined the pastry chefs in the kitchen readying more lemon tarts and raspberry mille-feuilles and peanut butter cheesecake brownies—an endless river of decadence.

In an instant, I was salivating. I was gripped by my cravings. My thoughts immediately turned to *what's in the fridge right now?!* And that was just from looking at the pictures and imagining I was there.

But I held on and next did what I knew would be very difficult in real life. In my mind, I turned myself around, and walked away. I headed for other parts of the restaurant with healthier, but equally delicious choices. I did this Innercise "mental rehearsal" over and over again, calling on my three neuro-muscles: awareness, intention, and action.

Here's a breakdown of the process:

- I used *awareness* to monitor my thoughts, feelings, and body sensations.

- When I noticed the trigger, and with practice, I was eventually able to choose to set my *intention* to eat healthier.

- Then I focused on my *action*—moving to a different part of the restaurant and choosing healthier yet still rewarding options—followed by an awareness of how being in more control and more empowered made me feel.

I repeated this Innercise several times a day during the weeks leading up to the trip. Each time, I used as much detail as possible, adding more sensory content to the images I'd found online. And each time, I interrupted the old habit loop and existing neural pattern in my brain and made a new habit loop—walk away and go find healthier dining.

When Robert and I arrived at the Encore in real life, we ended up eating at the restaurant every day. Without the advance mental rehearsal, I'm sure I would have consumed a frightening amount of sugar. But in my mind, I'd already been to the dessert bar forty times, and each trip up I turned around and walked away. In real life, all I did was walk away for the forty-first, forty-second, and forty-third time during our three-day stay.

It was a great moment for me. I had been able engage my conscious brain to direct my subconscious brain, instead of the other way around.

. . . .

INNERCISE: "I See Me" (Mental Rehearsal)

For this Innercise, start with calming down and getting centered:

"TAKE 6: Calm the Circuits"

Take six deep rhythmic breaths in through your nose and out through your mouth, like you are blowing out of a straw. As you breathe in, say,

I breathe in calmness, I breathe out stress.
or
I breathe in calmness, I breathe out fear.
or
I breathe in calmness, I breathe out anxiety, or overwhelm.

Now close your eyes and think of one goal you want to achieve. It doesn't matter how big or small it is but make it something you truly want to accomplish.

As you continue breathing calmly, in through your nose and out through your mouth, imagine that you've actually achieved that goal.

- What are you feeling knowing that you've arrived at this point of achievement?

- What sensations does it cause you to have in your body?

- Are there any colors associated with your accomplishment?

- Are there any people around you?

- Are there any animals, plants, or textures that come into your mind when you emotionalize and fully engage in your achievement?

The more you see your goal in your mind's eye and associate as many sensations, textures, colors, and sounds with your achievement, the more you will activate the motivational circuitry in your brain—the nucleus accumbens, insula, left prefrontal cortex—that can help you figure out the path to actually making the attainment of your goal a reality. And the more you rehearse the achievement of your goal in your mind, the more coherent your thoughts, emotions, and behaviors become in the process of achieving it.

Fine-Tuning Your Habit Hacking

Finding the main triggers and then replacing a behavior is a mechanism for changing unfavorable habits. It works, but it also takes effort. You won't beat most habits in one or two tries. Actually, research shows a wide range of time is usually needed, from 65 days to 365 days. But at NeuroGym, we like to use 100 days as a reasonable average to get a strong new habit pattern to develop and stick.

And though every person is unique, there are several reliable ways to increase your odds of success in changing your habits. Namely, through Innercise. Here are three of the best principles:

Principle 1: Make the Change Too Small to Fail

After studying human behavior for more than twenty years, B. J. Fogg, PhD, director of the Persuasive Tech Lab at Stanford University, claims there are only three ways to change your behavior in the long term: have an epiphany, change your environment, or take baby steps.[12]

The first one is hard to engineer. Epiphanies, by their nature, are difficult to do on demand. And changing your environment isn't always an option. As with your morning cup of coffee, you can't escape the environment of your kitchen, or a world filled with coffee drinkers and a Starbucks on every corner.

To help people with the third option, taking baby steps, Fogg developed the Tiny Habits method for making behavior change, and its basic premise is as simple as the name suggests: create habits by focusing on actions that are incredibly small.

Fogg uses flossing your teeth as an example. We all know we should floss our teeth daily, yet few do. Using Fogg's approach, we'd begin by simply flossing *one* tooth. That's right, just one.

Flossing one tooth is an action so brief and laughably simple that it's difficult to come up with any reasonable excuse for not doing it. Repeat that habit a few times, and then add a second tooth to the routine, and eventually, you have a new habit.

At a neurological level, the Tiny Habits approach taps into our reward system. A small success rewards us with dopamine, and as a result, we are more likely to repeat the behavior. The repetition, in turn, helps strengthen that neural pattern. Fogg's approach is based on the premise that *routine beats size*. Meaning you're better off to develop a regular routine of flossing a few teeth that you can build on, then to simply floss all of them once a year. Fogg argues that any other way to change your behavior requires willpower, and that's simply not a reliable way to build a sustainable habit.

Principle 2: Use Existing Habits to Build New Ones

What if we could use a good habit to help replace a bad one?

Let's say that you want to increase the amount you read. Perhaps you used to read a lot when you were younger, or maybe you'd like to learn more about a specific topic, but there never seems to be enough time to get through a book. If you could turn reading into a habit....

Well, you can. You can build a new habit by riding on the coattails of an existing one—a principle called *habit stacking*. Think about a habit you do daily, then use that *existing behavior as the trigger* for the habit you want to create. You're simply "stacking" the habit you want on to one that already exists.[13]

If your neurological habit loop for coffee is well entrained, for example, you can ride on those coattails, leveraging that existing neurological pattern to make your new habit easier to learn. Simply pour your cup of coffee as usual, and then head to your favorite chair with your book. Add Fogg's insight by committing to reading just a single page. Later, you'll find yourself reading two to three pages, and if the pleasure is there, perhaps reading for an hour or two a day.

Principle 3: Be Consistent

The biggest mistake people make in trying to change habits is not repeating the desired change often enough. Quite simply, you need to reinforce new behaviors to turn them into habits.

At first, you may find it easier to use *negative reinforcement* to help start your new habits—that means setting consequences for unfavorable behavior. Perhaps you make a contract, for example, so that each time you give in to the behavior you have to pay a friend $20.

Then once your new habit has gained momentum, you may find that *positive reinforcement* comes into play. Success with the new habit can become its own reward.[14] For example, exercising or eating well becomes fun for you.

You may also find it better to practice at a new habit every single day without fail. It may be easier, for example, to exercise seven days a week instead of three or four. Again, *routine is more important than size*. Or, as I often say, consistency is more important than intensity.

However, if you do "fall off the wagon," don't let it take you off course. Chalk it up to experience and get right back on the habit wagon.

Exercise: New Habit Formation

1. What small, new habit do you want to form, beginning today or tomorrow?

2. Can you "stack" this new habit on an existing positive, constructive pattern? Which one?

3. Write down one thing you can do to make it easier to practice this new habit, starting today or tomorrow.

4. At the end of the day, write down one sentence on how you succeeded.

Do not focus on anything negative that might undermine your efforts! Even if little changed, just write down one success story of the day, even the tiniest one, and one thing you feel grateful for.

Repeat this exercise for seven days and notice how your new habit is beginning to form. What excuses come up during this time? What resistance? What can you do to make sure you continue the new habit pattern?

Slip-Sliding Away: How Habits Decay

When it comes to success and reaching your goals, there are two ways to look at habits. There are disempowering habits; they're the ones that hold you back. And there are empowering habits; they're the ones that help you reach your full potential.

In reality, both types of habits are just patterns in the brain. Your subconscious brain doesn't judge habits as good or bad. As far as your brain is concerned, they're all equal. Your job then is to deliberately shift as many habits as possible to be ones that best serve you. Shift? You just woke up your gorilla.

It's also important to understand that your old habits never really die. Through long-term inactivity, they just get reduced essentially to a vegetative state in which the neural connections have degraded through a process called *synaptic decay*. If your old habits are highly pleasurable, addictive, or formed out of fear or trauma, it can take much longer to weaken those neural connections.

At a neurological level then, forming empowering habits is about creating new patterns of connections that become stronger with use, while the disempowering connections/ patterns slowly decay from lack of use. Here's a breakdown of the steps to accomplish this:

- Practice, rehearse, and repeat the desired behavior many times. Remember that habits are mental, emotional, and behavioral so you'll have to change more than just your actions.

- Continue repeating the behavior or attitude in novel ways to keep your brain interested and motivated.

- Take daily action, interrupt temptations, and persist until the empowering behavior begins to feel natural.

- Validate yourself for your accomplishment and for the benefits the new habit will bring.

Habits Are More Than Physical

Habits directing your thoughts and feelings are triggered in much the same way as your behavioral habits.

For example,

- A criticism from a coworker may trigger an angry outburst.

- An opportunity to attend a party with many new people may trigger an automatic thought of *I have to work the next day and need to sleep.*

- A wet towel left on the bedroom floor by someone you live with may lead to an instant feeling of resentment for having to do everything around the house.

In each case, disempowering habits are triggered, and you respond reflexively without even being aware of the slippery slope you've fallen in.

. . . .

INNERCISE: The Picture Frame

We live in a universe of dualities and polarities: For every up, there must be a down; for every inside, there must be an outside; for every good, there must be a bad; for every positive, there must be a negative. Yet, you can learn how to frame these dualities and polarities in favorable ways that empower you rather than drain you. Sort of a glass half-full or half-empty approach.

For example, throughout the day, notice when you are judging or experiencing your thoughts, emotions, feelings, or behaviors in a disempowering way. Notice when you label anything in your life in a disempowering way. If you can catch them, you can choose to change them.

Once you notice them, ask yourself: *What is right about this? What is positive here? How can I use this to grow? How can I use this to empower me?* What you will discover is that the meaning you choose to give something will determine how you feel about it and what you do or don't do about it.

Since your brain is a meaning-giving organism, the more you learn to frame things in ways that create rewarding meaning, the easier it can be to move forward victoriously.

In general, the process of shifting to a positive mindset is fed by *awareness and choice*. So, the stronger your awareness becomes, the stronger your empowering framing skills get.

. . . .

Real People. Real Results.

Emily was a single mother and a struggling business owner. For the first two and a half years, she didn't believe she'd ever be able to make a lot of money, but she gave it a shot anyway. For a long time, she was barely keeping her head above water:

"It's been a massive roller coaster of emotions playing on all my weaknesses, fears, and self-doubt. So many times, I've cried and cried and threatened to quit because it was too hard and hardly bringing in any money. But there was nothing that fitted as well with my chosen lifestyle, so I had to keep going."

She finally made the decision to commit to making her business work. She discovered Winning the Game of Money, an Innercise brain training program. Then, things really started to take off.

"John taught me that I needed to learn all the things I needed to learn. To learn about myself, my brain, how it works, and to understand how to control my emotions. To have faith in myself as a businesswoman, to learn how to run a successful business, how to market effectively. To not be afraid of money and start to manage it.

"Well, since January, all of last year's efforts are paying off. It's blowing my mind how easily my classes are filling up. Money is pouring in. Because I now keep accurate records I can see that I'll not only hit and exceed my goal… but it will be my highest income ever and today is only the ninth of the month!!!"

The biggest change for Emily was her mindset. She finally believed in herself and became committed to doing whatever it takes. After years of struggling, Emily is finally on the path to financial freedom and success.

Chapter Summary and Resources

Summary

- Habits mostly run beneath your awareness in your subconscious.

- Like addictions, habits get triggered and then operate on autopilot.

- Your brain doesn't recognize habits as good or bad. It only sees them as neural patterns.

- With consistent practice, you can change your disempowering habits into empowering ones.

Additional Free Resources

If you want additional help and free resources on how to best use each section in the book, I'm including some special coaching videos and 9 mini brain-training audios to go along with the book. I will act as your mindset coach as part of buying Innercise. For now, get started with this book and the free resources. Just scan the code below on your smartphone and log in to the NeuroGym platform or go to www.myneurogym.com/innercise to create a log in so you gain access to the free bonuses and resources.

Fear

From Fear to Fuel

"The cave you most fear to enter contains the greatest treasure."

—Joseph Campbell

In the summer of 2017, I sat in a San Diego hospital waiting for my name to be called. My appointment was for a routine MRI. But for me, even just sitting in the waiting room made me anxious. And when the white-coated technician called my name, I nearly jumped out of my seat in a panic and felt my heart race even more then it had been.

I couldn't explain all of the inner workings behind this at the time; however, I did know that since 9/11 I had developed a fear of being buried alive. Watching the news and seeing people saved after seven days underneath the rubble had left me with increasing anxiety about tightly enclosed spaces. So, when I was led into a white room dominated by that long, open-ended MRI cylinder, I felt like my already racing heart might just explode if it got pumping any faster.

At one level I knew this MRI scan would allow doctors to see inside my body and help treat a nagging shoulder injury

I'd gotten while skiing. But on another level, I saw it as an open mouth waiting to swallow me whole.

The procedure requires you to be slid inside the cylinder, which is so small that your elbows touch the sides and your nose is just a few inches from the uppermost curvature. If you're at all claustrophobic, then just hearing this description might speed up your heartbeat.

If, on the other hand, you're not afraid of confined spaces, you may be wondering *Why on earth would anyone be scared of this?* It's an excellent question, and certainly one I asked myself after I had finished and was safely outside.

Survival of the Scared-Est

Long before MRIs, back in our savannah-roaming, cave-dwelling days, the world was indeed a very dangerous place. To survive, humans had to be cautious. Threats abounded: predators, poisonous foods, insects, dangerous weather, and starvation.

Under these conditions, those who were the most sensitive to threats—strange sounds, unusual smells, sudden movements, angry creatures, and more—tended to live longer and reproduce more often. As a result, over millions of years, evolution gave our brain a very sensitive system for detecting and responding to potential danger.

Today, you likely won't face down an angry beast, but the same threat-detection areas of the brain are active, and they continue to be triggered by anything perceived as risk, ranging from limited phobias such as public speaking, heights, and enclosed spaces to far-reaching, life-limiting feelings such as a sense of shame, loneliness, and failure.

This system is so sensitive, so fast, and so effective that it takes precedent over almost all your other systems. It can hijack your heart and change your hormones. It can affect your vision and change your breathing. When you face a perceived threat—whether it's truly threatening or not, real or imagined—*the part of your brain that controls fear takes charge.*

This is the system that was activated in me when I faced the MRI machine. The closer I got to it, the more the fear circuitry in my brain lit up. My already elevated pulse began to pound in my ears. My vision narrowed. And as I was slid, headfirst, into the narrow tube of the machine, I teetered on the brink of panic.

Fight, Flight, or Freeze: How Fear Works in the Brain

What was going on in my brain at that moment is something that happens in yours too when your brain perceives a threat. Here's a snapshot of what I call a fear circuit. This term makes it easy to visualize the process; however, there isn't actually a structural fear circuit in the brain.

1. Input from the senses, like the sight of the confining MRI machine, is relayed to every part of your brain. In my case, my brain said, "Hey…this is confined space and I think I'm going to get stuck…or die!"

2. The interpretation areas in the brain—those based on past memories, fears, beliefs, and habits—add context to the situation by comparing your present against your past, and then pass information to the *amygdala.*

3. The amygdala determines whether this is a true threat. The amygdala is a big player in the fear game. It

processes many memories relating to past threats and painful experiences and it tells the rest of your brain what action to take.

Faced with even a hint of pain or danger or disappointment, you'll move into one of the following four modes:

- *Fight* the threat
- *Flee* from the threat
- *Freeze* in place or
- *Faint* as a result of too much electro-chemical stimuli

Using the example with me and the MRI machine,

- I looked for escape routes, so I could *flee*.

- I thought about bracing my legs against the machine to *fight* against being put inside.

- And in the end? I *froze*, and they slid me inside.

I suppose some consolation is at least I didn't faint. But had I been a caveman facing a saber-toothed tiger, I would have been toast.

Later, I'll explain how I used specific Innercises to take control of my fear, and how future MRIs became easy. But in that moment my fear response was fully activated. I was frozen with fear.

Whether you think of yourself as brave or fearful or somewhere in between, you have this same basic brain wiring as surely as you have a heart. This system is so essential, so vital for your survival that *everything* you encounter in the external world—even what you are aware of and what hides in your subconscious—passes through this fear system, "theoretically" to keep you safe.

Time and time again, your brain weighs and assesses risks. It compares what you sense and think and feel against your memories and unconscious thoughts to watch for danger— real *or* perceived.

. . . .

INNERCISE: I Release

Start with a slight variation on Innercise #1, Take 6 Calm the Circuits. As you take six gentle breathes in through your nose and out through your mouth, it is important for you to check in with how serious you are about finally letting go of anything that has held you back in the past. In order for this Innercise to be effective, you must be ready to allow this to work.

"TAKE 6: Calm the Circuits"

Take six deep rhythmic breaths in through your nose and out through your mouth, like you are blowing out of a straw. As you breathe in, say,

I breathe in calmness, I breathe out stress.
or
I breathe in calmness, I breathe out fear.
or
I breathe in calmness, I breathe out anxiety, or overwhelm.

Now think about what you are ready to release. It can be a disempowering belief. An event that traumatized you. A person who is affecting you in a negative way. A job or relationship that is holding you back. A fear that is holding you hostage. A habit that is destructive. The stress you are feeling. It can be anything.

But you must be ready to say it, feel it, and do it. So, choose one thing and really feel yourself committed to releasing it.

Now breathe in and say the following (fill in the blank) affirmation:

I am now ready to release _____ and so I am.

Repeat this over and over again ten times with conviction, emotion, and certainty.

When you are ready, imagine what it would feel like if this release really was true—that you really were releasing this one thing holding you back.

Thinking it, saying it, feeling it, and repeating it conditions your brain to make it a reality and it will especially help you when you do the next part of this Innercise.

Name one small action step you can take to make your release more real than just repeating the affirmation.

Whatever this is, do it today, now. Teach yourself that no matter what has happened in the past or what may be happening now, today is the day you can change and become more of who you want to be because you are finally ready. DO IT! This will build your confidence. Make small, powerful decisions that you follow through on daily and soon enough you will release whatever you have decided needs to go.

The REAL Challenge of Fear

It's easy for us to point to things we're consciously fearful of, like deep water or snakes. Or clowns—seriously, it's called coulrophobia. But a fear of snakes or clowns isn't likely to stand in the way of your dreams.

Your fear response is governed in gorilla territory—it's fast and subconscious. Information from your senses reaches the amygdala, the big player in the fear circuit, *almost twice as fast* as it reaches your frontal lobes where you become conscious of it. That means your ancient brain can already be well on its way to Amityville before your present-day, conscious brain can even put its pants on.

In fact, the amygdala is nicknamed the "smoke detector" of your brain. It's designed to go off at the slightest whiff of trouble—a "fear first, ask questions later" system that ensures you err on the side of caution.

In modern life, however, as with smoke detectors, *there are a lot of false alarms.* Even though you're not actually faced with daily survival threats like attacks from woolly mammoths, your ancient fear system is still constantly scanning and reacting as if mammoths could trample you in an instant.

In fact, most of your fears are based on old memories, which can be perceived as present-day threats by the amygdala and other threat detection mechanisms spread throughout deeper structures of the brain. This means you can be afraid at a neurological level more often than you realize. And that can have a dramatic negative impact on your life.

For example,

- Your coworker may not have sharp teeth or carry a club, but your brain may still see him as an alarming threat based on his angry glance, his competitive posture, or his offhand remarks about you.

- An upcoming sales contest literally won't mean life or death for the victor, but your brain may still see it as a high-stakes competition.

- Your credit card bill can't suffocate you like a boa constrictor, but your brain may see it as squeezing you to the point of loss of breath if you don't have the money to pay it.

This Is Your Life on Fear

Fear is valuable. Let's be clear on that. All of the talk you may hear about "being fearless" and to live your life to the fullest is ridiculous. Aside from its obvious survival function as we have been discussing, you need fear to thrive, to realize your highest potential. Risks versus rewards are constants in life, so you better have a healthy respect for fear or you could get hammered with every risk, no matter how small the calculation may be. Driving to the store to pick up a gallon of milk would seem to be an extremely low risk decision, with likely no fear whatsoever arising. But if you text while driving and no fear arises, you could get killed, or, worse, kill an innocent bystander.

The distinction I want to make then has more to do with discerning between rational and irrational fears. Rational ones are healthy. Listen to them. Assess them, and then decide on your course of action. The other ones, the irrational ones that are constant and keep you in a state of vigilance and crisis response mode, are quite often real barriers though.

Let's say that you stuttered when giving a speech in high school English, and your classmates laughed at you. You were embarrassed, maybe even humiliated. Because your subconscious mind's job is to learn what situations are dangerous or painful, and to protect you from similar dangers in the future, it takes note of the strong feelings associated with those exposures. In this example, your subconscious takes note and classifies public speaking as a danger.

Years later, as an adult, you realize that if you start speaking more publicly it will raise your profile, get your message out into the world, attract business opportunities and influence, get you some of the recognition you deserve, and more. Your conscious mind holds the goal of speaking publicly, but your subconscious says, *High school English class. The horror! Never again!*

What's happening? Your subconscious mind has resorted to one of the three ancient response mechanisms. Its intention is to keep you safe and free of emotional and physical pain. But as the saying goes, "The road to hell is paved with good intentions." So instead of reaping the rewards from going out there and doing more public speaking, you end up doing one of the following:

- *Taking flight* by wiggling out of any speaking engagements you have already agreed to and coming up with stories of why you can't agree to more

- *Fighting* your way out of the situation by becoming difficult and demanding, which your subconscious mind hopes will get you released from the obligation

- *Freezing* so that you are cut off from speaking engagement opportunities

- *Fainting* due to the intense neurochemical release from your skyrocketing anxiety

Even though you may have graduated from high school twenty-five years ago, your fear of being embarrassed and humiliated may seem as though it happened yesterday. In your subconscious mind, the wound is still too fresh—even twenty-five years later—and it tells you you're not ready, and may never be ready, to successfully engage in public speaking, no matter what you do or how hard you work.

So, when this irrational fear triggers an old memory in your brain, you most likely will stop doing what you want to do, need to do, to reach your goals, and instead unconsciously go rogue. For example,

- *Fear causes you to unknowingly procrastinate.* Instead of taking action, you do something else nonthreatening and familiar to help relieve your anxiety and tension, unaware that the procrastination creates its own new set of anxieties and tensions.

- *Fear causes you to self-sabotage.* Because fear drives blood to the brain and fires learned patterns, it changes the way you think and make decisions. It causes doubt and uncertainty. It greatly impairs your conscious ability to make careful evaluations as your resources are shifted toward fighting, fleeing, freezing, or fainting; to remain optimistic as it shuts down the mindfulness circuitry in your left prefrontal cortex;[15] and to make wise decisions as it excites tendencies to run away with yourself in the imagination centers of your frontal lobes.

• Your subconscious fears (along with the worrisome thoughts generated by the imagination centers in your frontal lobes) will shatter your chances for success by causing you to move away from the actions you must take to achieve success.

• *Fear inhibits your inner genius.* When your brain is in fear mode, your higher brain functions are inhibited as your resources are shifted toward fighting, fleeing, or freezing.

• *Fear inhibits your optimism and decision-making processes.* Research shows that when your fears, negative feelings, and emotions are stimulated, they shut down the optimism and decision-making circuits in your left prefrontal cortex.[16]

• *Fear causes you to unknowingly rationalize your way out of what you know you should be doing.* I like to break up the word rationalize into two words: *Rational-lies.* You tell yourself and others rational lies as to why you don't want to do something or why you won't.

What makes these irrational fears all the more challenging is that the triggers for your fear response can be set off by a lack of knowledge or skill, by something you read, or heard, or saw on a screen. The result is when you feel fear, parts of your brain are more active; blood flow increases to those parts of the brain. That, in turn, limits blood flow to other parts of the brain. So, when you're afraid, your fear center can literally take over the rest of your brain.

That means unresolved, subconscious fear can bleed into your life, impacting everything from your income to your relationships and physical health. When you let the fear circuit take control, you surrender.

In a NeuroGym survey, we asked more than 90,000 people what their top fears were—what was holding them back the most from achieving the life they wanted.

They revealed hundreds of different fears. People were afraid of failure…and afraid of success. They were afraid of rejection…and afraid of being alone. They were afraid of not being smart enough…and afraid of being too smart! For every person, there was a fear—truth be told, each had many fears.

Turning unhealthy fears to your advantage begins when you can recognize the ways they hold you back. It's the first step to releasing their grip and breaking through to the next level of success in your life.

Exercise: Identify Your Fears

Which of the fears below and on the next page resonates with you? Choose the one or two that you feel most often stand in the way of you reaching your full potential.

- Fear of failure
- Fear of success
- Fear of looking foolish
- Fear of public speaking

- Fear of loneliness
- Fear of poverty
- Fear of being unloved
- Fear of disappointment
- Fear of being judged
- Fear of change
- Fear of being ashamed
- Fear of being embarrassed
- Fear of rejection
- Fear of the unknown
- Fear of being overwhelmed
- Fear of taking action
- Fear of losing freedom
- Fear of making mistakes
- Fear of being hurt
- Fear of losing everything
- Fear of being ridiculed
- Fear of not being good enough
- Fear of not being smart enough
- Fear of taking action
- Fear of being alone
- Fear of being helpless
- Fear of change
- Fear of circumstances
- Fear of complacency
- Fear of corruption
- Fear of running out of time
- Fear of what others think
- Fear of loss of self
- Fear of not belonging
- Fear of being a fraud
- Fear of attracting attention

The True Cost of Fear

Look at the number one fear you identified in the exercise above and consider the following:

1. What could you accomplish now if you were free of your number one fear?

2. What career or business decisions have you made that you would make differently now if you were free of your number one fear?

3. What potential relationship with a special person did you look away from? What unhealthy relationship have you stayed in because of your number one fear?

Now try this exercise by inserting other fears that have held you back and continue to hold you back from achieving your true potential.

If you're honest in your responses, considering these questions can be a painful process. Fortunately, with Innercise you can retrain your brain to not only deal with acute, conscious fears like being afraid of heights and enclosed spaces but also with subconscious, debilitating fears associated with failure, loneliness, and rejection.

From One Small Space to Another

After my disastrous MRI experience, I was determined to beat my fear and claustrophobia. After all, I knew I wasn't going to be able to avoid enclosed spaces for the rest of my life.

So, I chose to confront it in a way that would give me more control over managing my fear response. The answer was a very specific Innercise sequence.

Not long after my MRI, I booked an appointment to spend time in a floatation tank. If you aren't familiar with flotation tanks, they're enclosed, pitch-black chambers partly filled with salt water. Floatation tanks allow you to float in utter silence and darkness, your body weight supported by the dense salt water. The tank's environment removes a huge amount of the sensory input you normally get in each moment of each day; thus, it makes for a great place to meditate and soothe an overactive mind.

Even knowing all of this beforehand, just the thought of climbing into the tank was enough to fire up my fear response. So, I began with the following two Innercises.

First, Take 6

When your fear response is active, it's tough to focus on anything else. That's why the first Innercise for fear management and mastery is the Take 6: Calm the Circuits breathing exercise from earlier.

"TAKE 6: Calm the Circuits"

Take six deep rhythmic breaths in through your nose and out through your mouth, like you are blowing out of a straw. As you breathe in, say,

I breathe in calmness, I breathe out stress.

or

I breathe in calmness, I breathe out fear.

or

I breathe in calmness, I breathe out anxiety, or overwhelm.

Next, follow these steps:

1. When you start to feel anxiety, or fear, stop what you're doing, observe the experience, and deepen your awareness of your emotions and sensations—*don't fight this.*

2. Take in six, long, gentle breaths through your nose and out through your mouth for 60 seconds. When blowing out through your mouth do it as if you are blowing out through a straw. Feel the stress neurochemicals leave your body. Imagine that you're inhaling calm and exhaling little "clouds" of fear.

3. Repeat if necessary. Six breaths are often the magic number for calming down when you're in an excited state. If you're still anxious, however, *keep breathing for one to two more minutes.*

Once you've calmed down, smile. You've shifted from your fear "fight or flight" response system to your "relax and respond" system. You just transformed your fear!

Once I had subdued my fear, I was able to climb into the tank. At that point, I repeated the Innercise with the tank door open, until I was ready to close the lid and float in darkness. And while inside, as needed, I continued to do the Innercise, plus this next one—a favorite of mine—Beach Time.

. . . .

INNERCISE: Beach Time

This Innercise can be used anytime you are feeling stressed or fearful and you just need a little time to escape the disempowering emotion. It's a form of distraction therapy that can be an excellent tool for when you need a temporary mental and emotional break.

Start with the Take 6: Calm the Circuits breathing exercise.

"TAKE 6: Calm the Circuits"

Take six deep rhythmic breaths in through your nose and out through your mouth, like you are blowing out of a straw. As you breathe in, say,

I breathe in calmness, I breathe out stress.
or
I breathe in calmness, I breathe out fear.
or
I breathe in calmness, I breathe out anxiety, or overwhelm.

- As you become aware of the flow of your breath, of your body calming down, imagine that you are standing barefoot with your feet on firm, warm sand; you are on the most beautiful beach you have ever seen.

- It can be a beach that you have in memory from one you have visited in the past, or it can be what a perfect beach would look like in your mind's eye.

- As you look left, you see beautiful palm trees and the most perfectly colored sand. As you look in front of you, the waves are crashing in such a way that you instantly feel relaxed, connected, and at peace. As you look to the right, you notice some sea life playing on top of the water, and as you look closer, it appears that there are a couple of dolphins swimming around, playing in the water.

- As you walk along the sand, you notice a cabana. You walk toward it and discover that on a small stand there is a cold drink to quench your thirst. As you sit back in the lounge chair, breathing in and breathing out, you remember what it feels like to be totally relaxed and calm as the waves gently roll in. The warm wind on your face feels so soothing and the sun warming up your skin is just perfect. Not too hot, not too cold, just perfect and exactly what you need right now to get you centered and aware of this magical place and time.

- As you continue inhaling and exhaling you remember how good it feels to stop and just be. Relaxed, calm, and in the present moment.

- Keep breathing in and out gently.

You can do this short Innercise any time you want to get grounded and centered as you give yourself a little reprieve from life's daily grind.

. . . .

Each time I felt my fear response kick in while I was in the flotation tank, I turned my attention to the Take 6 Innercise to calm myself. The Beach Escape Innercise then took my mind away to an amazing beach in the British Virgin Islands.

By combining the Take 6 and Beach Time Innercises into a "stack," within seconds I was able to be whisked away from my fears and into a blissful state of calm.

After a few of these successes, I began to test myself. I imagined that I wasn't in a floatation tank anymore...no, but in a coffin! And that I was buried alive! Almost immediately, my breathing and heart rate increased, and I felt the familiar, early twinges of panic. Instead of frantically pushing open the tank door, however, I did the "Take 6: Calm the Circuits" Innercise again.

Soon, I regained my inner calm and once more imagined I was buried alive.

When I felt my fear rise, I calmed myself. I also used the AiA Innercise over and over again to show myself that I could override any emotion or feeling that was unpleasant or downright scary.

With practice, this "flip-flopping" of Innercises, which I'll detail later, allowed me to turn my fear response on and off like a light switch. I made several visits to the floatation tank facility, each time practicing the "flip-flop" with variations on the buried alive scenario.

Weeks later, I returned for a follow-up MRI and waited in the same room. Only this time I felt far more in control. Any time I felt nervous, I would calm myself by breathing just like I had in the tank.

A short time later the same white-coated technician from before slid me into the narrow tube of the MRI machine.

Yikes! It was immediately clear that my fear hadn't vanished. As I lay inside the tube, the sides pressing against me, I felt my heart rate climb, and the familiar panic rise. This time, however, I was prepared. I went back to doing the Innercises and almost immediately became calmer; I could sense that my heart rate and autonomic stress responses were normal.

Not only did I make it through the 25-minute MRI session with hardly a dent, I felt almost euphoric that I had changed my brain and had well-managed my emotions.

Using Fear as Fuel

Is fear a bad thing?

For most of our lives, our default state is to move away from anything causing fear. In the case of real danger, this makes sense. If you don't move away from real risk, you'll have a short life.

Most risks we face shouldn't scare us as much as they do, yet, who hasn't choked when

- Talking to a stranger
- Asking for money
- Speaking in public
- Learning new skills
- Inviting someone new out on a date

There's little or no rational reason to be afraid then. We are though, usually because, at a subconscious level, the meaning we have associated with talking to a stranger, or whatever else we want or need to do, suggests the potential for real pain or discomfort. The more often you can face those types of fears and come out the other side, the stronger you will be, the more confidence you'll build, and the closer you'll be to your dreams. In fact, these are *necessary steps on the path to your highest potential.* Which means fear can be a signpost.

What if every time you experienced an irrational fear—one that wasn't life-threatening—you chose to move *toward* it instead of away from it? What if you viewed fear not as an obstacle, but as a way to strengthen your confidence and emotional mastery?

Every time you strengthen your emotional neuro-muscles, it becomes that much easier to overcome these fears the next time you feel them and, in the process, develop new self-respect, new self-love, and new inner strength.

The key is to recognize these irrational fears immediately, understand their nature, and stop them before they develop into habitual patterns.

So, the next time you feel anxious, or are holding back from a new experience or a step toward your goals, take six deep breaths and ask yourself, *Is my fear trying to show me something important?*

Real People. Real Results.

Sandhya was an artist and coach who had spent most of her life living in fear. The memories of her abusive childhood destroyed her confidence and stopped her from promoting herself and her art shows. Her business was suffering because every time she thought about working on her website or inviting people to her exhibitions, the crippling fear of being judged came crashing down upon her.

She explains: "Being 'not good enough' always meant being punished severely. When my parents thought I could have done better and I didn't live up to their expectations I used to get beaten up by my dad: fists, leather belts, branches of trees, glass—whatever was on hand. I have sabotaged myself over and over again by running away and hiding—hiding myself, hiding my art, hiding my abilities."

This kind of self-sabotage was especially evident whenever she took action toward promoting herself or her business. She describes the immediate feelings that overtook her moments after sending out an email to her list: "I sent out an email inviting people to an exhibition I've got coming up and found out later I had invited a couple of people whom I hold in very high regard. Immediately I started cringing inside and I went into panic mode. My thoughts were 'Oh, no…they'll think I'm an idiot. They'll laugh at me. They'll think I'm a stupid person who doesn't know what she is doing.' I felt like I was going to be judged and found to be not good enough."

Once Sandhya engaged in her daily practice of Innercising, when she felt these painful emotions appear, she was able to stay calm and get control of them and get back on track.

"Interestingly the Innercise I've been listening to the most has been about releasing stories and excuses and letting go of what has been holding me back. Through this process, I realized I have always sought approval from others in order for me to move forward. Whenever I haven't had this approval I would avoid any danger that comes from doing something that is deemed 'not good enough.' The process of Innercising has set off a chain reaction where I can finally heal and let go of the emotional baggage that used to hold me back. I'm looking forward to interesting changes and different action steps. Here's to a whole new beginning."

Sandhya committed herself to a whole new vision for what her life can be. One where her past stories and traumas didn't control her future.

Chapter Summary and Resources

Summary

- Most fears are "patterns in the subconscious vault" of your life experiences. They can be born from both real and imagined experiences.

- You can subconsciously feel fearful without ever consciously being aware of it.

- Irrational, subconscious fears can have a huge cost to your health, wealth, and happiness.

Additional Free Resources

If you want additional help and free resources on how to best use each section in the book, I'm including some special coaching videos and 9 mini brain-training audios to go along with the book. I will act as your mindset coach as part of buying Innercise. For now, get started with this book and the free resources. Just scan the code below on your smartphone and log in to the NeuroGym platform or go to www.myneurogym.com/innercise to create a log in so you gain access to the free bonuses and resources.

Beliefs and Stories

From Limiting Tales to Powerful Epics

> *"Man often becomes what he believes himself to be...if I have the belief that I can do it, I shall surely acquire the capacity to do it even if I may not have it at the beginning."*
>
> —Mahatma Gandhi

If there's one question I've been asked more than any other over the years, it's "How can I make more money?"

From single parents below the poverty line to millionaires, from farmers to coders, almost everyone wants to know how they can increase their income and have more security.

What's most notable is the question itself. In addition to asking, "How can I earn more?" you need to also ask, "Why am I stuck where I am?" Because this simplistic view that financial security equates to overall security is false. In fact, a wide range of studies conclusively show that beyond a certain level of income that meets basic needs plus offers a healthy cushion—at the time of this publication that ranges from about $55,000 to $85,000 in annual income for an American family of four, depending on the study and where the family lives, i.e., the South has a lower cost of living than the West—real happiness does not increase. The studies reveal that a baseline of happiness is about the same for someone making $70,000 a year as someone making $10 million a year. The adage that money can't buy happiness has scientific backing behind it. Whereas feeling stuck, no matter how much you have in the bank, has a direct bearing on your happiness and sense of fulfillment and purpose in life.

I first faced these questions in my late teens when I decided against going to college and continued searching for answers through my early twenties. I was determined to change my life, and it seemed as if I was off to a great start in selling real estate. In addition to having clear goals and guidance from wonderful mentors, I worked my butt off for those commission-only sales. And for the first time in a long time, I felt hopeful and energized.

There was just one problem: My results didn't match my goals. I was making money, but I wasn't getting even close to where I'd thought I'd be. Worse still, almost everyone else in my branch office seemed to be doing better than me. Not just in terms of outperforming and earning bigger commissions, but also in not working as hard.

I suspect you've been in a similar situation at some point. You have big plans and take big actions, yet reality smacks you with disappointing results that fall well short of your vision.

What I discovered was that my "stuck-ness" had little to do with the real estate market, my sales skills, or the competition, and everything to do with my *beliefs*. Specifically, my hidden beliefs.

How Your Beliefs Shape Your Reality

The placebo effect, where someone seemingly experiences a positive result from a treatment or program just from believing in it, is quite real. For example, taking what you believe is medicine but, in reality, is just a sugar pill may reduce the pain of a headache, arthritis, or any number of conditions. In fact, the average placebo effect is 33 percent—though it can be higher or lower depending on the medical condition; for instance, patients with depression are much more susceptible to placebo effects than patients with generalized pain. The placebo effect is even present in some surgeries. Our beliefs about the power of these medical treatments have a measurable impact on our physical body.

But the placebo effect goes well beyond sugar pills making you feel better. Here are just a few examples of how other beliefs can actually result in a wide range of real-world improvements:

- If you believe that the work you're doing is good exercise, that belief alone is enough to make you lose weight.[17]

- Believing you look younger can change your blood pressure and give you a vitality that leads other people to believe you're younger too.[18]

- If you believe some amounts of stress are good for you, you can be happier, more productive, and less impacted by fatigue and other negative consequences from burdensome stress.[19]

- Growing evidence suggests that your beliefs about aging can affect how long you live![20]

The lesson of all this is profound: *Beliefs help form your reality, drive your behavior, and shape your destiny.* And that means, instead of just asking how to earn more money, for example, ask, "What beliefs do I have about myself and my ability to rise up to my fullest potential, including earning more money?"

How Beliefs Work in the Brain

For all their impressive power, beliefs are, in essence, habits—habits of automatically thinking in particular ways—and, so, are just patterns of brain activity caused by neural connections that have been reinforced over time by our experiences. The real ones and the imagined ones. They're often old memories stored in the brain, and, like most brain patterns, they can cause us to view the world without thinking through a process called automaticity.

Once beliefs are established, they can become even more powerful as your brain continues to look for evidence to support your position. Researchers refer to this as confirmation bias. For example, if you believe *I'm unlucky*, you'll tend to ruminate on *the time it rained the whole week of my tropical vacation; the time I lost my job right after I bought a new house; the time I got dumped on Christmas Eve* rather than when you were quite lucky: *I missed getting piled up in that car accident by a few seconds; I get to work from home now and make more than I ever have; I've got good friends who are like family to me.* This tendency can make beliefs become self-fulfilling prophecies, and thus perpetuate the cycle.

Over time, beliefs can become so entrenched that they color not just how we see ourselves, but how we see the world. As an example, an entire population of a certain race, ethnicity, gender, age, socio-economic level can be dangerously mischaracterized to fit a prejudicial narrative. Beliefs are, in effect, a *story*, and that story comes to define what we believe to be true and drives the behaviors that create our results.

What Beliefs ARE

- Things you feel certain about and have references for
- Developed filters through which you see yourself and the world
- Neural patterns in your brain that have been reinforced
- Stories you tell about yourself and the world
- Changeable!

What Your Beliefs are NOT

- Things you were born with
- Always easily identifiable
- Always the truth
- Permanent!

When I first learned about beliefs as a young man, it seemed straightforward enough: If I wanted to increase my income, I just had to *believe* I could. What could be simpler? The problem was I *already* believed I could earn more money, yet it wasn't happening. So, after a lot of self-reflection, I came to realize I didn't know what I didn't know.

It turned out that with beliefs, like just most everything else related to the mind, there are those we're aware of, and those we aren't.

Two Types of Beliefs

The conscious/subconscious divide in your brain creates two types of beliefs: those that are *explicit* and those that are *implicit*.

Explicit beliefs are ones you are conscious of. You can articulate them. When you say, "I'm going to become a millionaire," that's an explicit belief.

An implicit belief though is largely subconscious. You might, for example, have a deeply hidden belief such as "I'm not smart enough to be a millionaire."

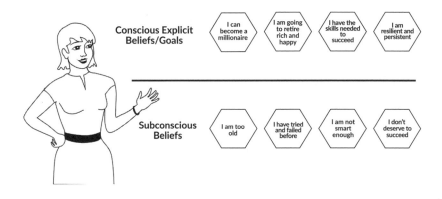

Remember, your brain wants alignment between your consciousness and subconsciousness. It requires this balance for a perception of safety and efficiency. When we have conflicting beliefs, behaviors, or perceptions, we can experience what is referred to as *cognitive dissonance*. For example, if you smoke (and frankly at this point who doesn't know it's bad for you?), you likely experience cognitive dissonance. Even when you aren't consciously aware of a misalignment, you can still experience cognitive dissonance. For example, after you have a smoke your intimate partner pulls away from kissing you for a time, though their retreat is imperceptible to you. When your explicit and implicit beliefs don't "agree," you can begin to lose brain coherence. And when this happens, your brain will default to your subconscious beliefs and habits in an effort to squash the conflict and bring your mind back into alignment.

That's right. Your *subconscious beliefs will almost always win.* Your conscious brain may be able to hold the high ground for a time—you might take the first steps toward a new business, for example, or toward better communication in your relationships—but unless you structurally change your subconscious belief patterns, you'll eventually slip back into those old ways.

Now going back to my early years when I was trying to build my real estate business, consciously, I believed I could earn millions. I wrote out affirmations and read them every morning as I moved my fingers across each sentence. I sat quietly in my office chair and imagined what my life would be like. I would mentally and emotionally rehearse receiving awards, getting praised in public, and then sharing how I achieved my goals. Daily, *I opened myself to the abundance of the universe. I repeated my affirmations over and over again. Money is flowing to me easily and effortlessly. I deserve great wealth. Being prosperous is my divine right.* I read all the classics like *Think and Grow Rich, The Richest Man in Babylon,* and *As a Man Thinketh.* I subscribed to the *Wall Street Journal* and I started to read daily about achieving success. I listened to audio training cassette tapes over and over again for hundreds of hours until I could repeat every word that was being said.

However, subconsciously, something very different was going on. Namely an implicit belief that I wasn't smart enough. That my dad was right. He had warned me, "If you skip college you'll be a slave to your job and barely eke out a living." *Maybe I wasn't smart enough. I've never done well in school so that speaks for itself about my intelligence.* So, while I believed consciously that I could learn how to make money, subconsciously, I felt I didn't have the brains to get it done.

This difference meant my self-esteem took a regular pounding, despite whatever success I did have in real estate. As a result, I sabotaged my success. I procrastinated. I hid under the covers to keep safe from affluent clients and connections who were upper class or highly intelligent because they were too scary for me. In the end, I did fewer sales. And those sales were in the lower price ranges.

As I became aware of these implicit beliefs, I learned how to deal with them. That was my first real introduction to Innercise, though I didn't know it at the time. As I began to let go of my old implicit beliefs and create powerful new ones, my income began to skyrocket.

This insight into the explicit and implicit nature of beliefs helped explain a great deal about why I struggled with making change. And I believe it can help you understand yourself better too. Think about this…

- Why do most lottery winners lose it all and end up right back at the level of wealth they started with?

- Why do dieters lose weight only to gain it back and end up right back at the weight they started at?

- Why do some people sabotage their own success just when they start to earn more?

The answer is a conflict in conscious and subconscious beliefs. Fortunately, brain science now has insight into beliefs at a neural level.

Where Beliefs Live in the Brain

The likely central reason why you're stuck earning an income you're not happy with has far less to do with your intellect, talent, or who you know, and much more to do with you being conditioned to accept a certain amount of income. You could think of this as your financial set point, similar to your happiness set point that I discussed in the last chapter.

When your income—perceived or real—differs from your financial set point, an alarm goes off in the hypothalamus part of your brain where homeostasis is maintained. And just like an air conditioner/heater thermostat, your hypothalamus will bring you back to where you're comfortable—your financial set point—by turning up or down the temperature of your thoughts, emotions, and behaviors without you even realizing it.

You'll then likely automatically rationalize why you don't need more money. Or if you do, you'll rationalize why it's not worth what you'd have to give up to get it—"I like my freedom. I don't want to be tied down." Or, "My path is to be true to myself. I'm too spiritual for the material world." Or, "Why would I want to end up being a slave to my possessions? Less is more." *Rationalize?* More like *rational lies!*

. . . .

Innercise: Identify Your Limiting Beliefs

The first part of changing your beliefs is to identify the ones holding you back. Set aside fifteen minutes to complete this Innercise. For best results, use the "TAKE 6: Calm the Circuits" Innercise first.

"TAKE 6: Calm the Circuits"

Take six deep rhythmic breaths in through your nose and out through your mouth, like you are blowing out of a straw. As you breathe in, say,

I breathe in calmness, I breathe out stress.
or
I breathe in calmness, I breathe out fear.
or
I breathe in calmness, I breathe out anxiety, or overwhelm.

1. Go through the list below and identify any that res-
    onate with you. If you think of a related belief about
    money, add it to your list.
    -   Rich people are greedy.
    -   I'm not a people person.
    -   Being successful takes too much time.
    -   You have to work more to earn more.
    -   Money doesn't grow on trees.
    -   I'm too old to start a business/change jobs.
    -   Rich people are insincere.
    -   I can't change because of my genes.
    -   You have to have money to make money.

- I don't have the connections to earn more.
- I don't have time for _____.
- I'm afraid of_____.
- People won't like me if I'm successful.
- Work isn't fun—that's just the way life is.
- I'm not the entrepreneur type.
- You can't get a good job without a college degree.
- I'll never be able to afford that.
- I'm not a salesperson.
- Marketing is aggressive and intrusive.
- You need to be unethical to get ahead.
- Successful people burn out.
- Making money just means more hassles.

Which of these beliefs is holding you back? Rank these from most to least.

. . . .

Realigning Your Beliefs

Once you've identified the beliefs that are holding you back, your job is to retrain your brain so that your implicit beliefs align with your explicit ones. Here are four strategies to help you create these new, empowering implicit beliefs:

1. Tap into Your Creative Brain

John Lennon was a rowdy seventeen-year-old, chasing girls, ditching school, living for rock 'n' roll and his band named the Quarry Men, when he went ahead and took a chance in July 1957 on bringing into his band more of a polished type: fifteen-year-old Paul McCartney. Before they had known each other—though it seemed like everyone knew of John, including Paul who idolized this older kid with all that swagger—separately they had dabbled at writing music. Neither had any real encouragement. In fact, neither personally knew any songwriters and didn't take their own musings too seriously. A few months later, toward the end of 1957, separately, John wrote *Hello Little Girl* and Paul wrote *I Lost My Little Girl.*

The similarity in their titles was of less interest to them than the similarity in their sounds. How these two came up with remarkably complimentary harmonies while off writing by themselves gave them an epiphany. It was John who pushed it. After all it was his band. He said later, "Practically every Buddy Holly song was three chords, so why not write your own?" Buddy—the icon, the god—was the biggest name in the world, well, along with Elvis Presley. And so, they gave it a try.

Paul described their first attempt at collaborating: "We'd sit down and say, 'OK, what are we going to do?' and we'd just start off strumming and one or the other of us would kick off some kind of idea and then we'd just develop it and bounce off each other." *Too Bad About Sorrows* was their first, but it never went anywhere. Maybe never even got finished and just a few of the lines have ever surfaced: "Too bad about sorrows, too bad about love, there'll be no tomorrow, for all of your life."

"Kicking off some kind of idea" is how many of history's greatest minds, from Newton to Einstein to Jobs arrived at world-changing breakthroughs. Whether through stepping back to get a wider perspective, or daydreaming, or brainstorming, or whatever process worked for them, they found ways to stimulate their creative juices. But here's the good news, you don't have to be famous; particularly talented, let alone gifted; incredibly smart; or anything else to tap into the same process. This creative domain lives in each of us. It is a birthright. Admittedly some can access their creativity more easily than others, but it's always there in everyone.

According to neuroscience researchers Mark Waldman and Dr. Andrew Newberg, one of the first steps in creating new beliefs is to follow in those "Eureka!" footsteps by increasing your imagination. When you deliberately and consciously focus on a bigger idea or vision, you inhibit your limiting beliefs by increasing activity and motivation in the frontal lobes of your brain.

You've already experienced this when you had an "aha" moment in the shower, or perhaps while driving, and from somewhere invisible a great idea, a long sought-after answer, a hidden problem that needs fixing, pops into your head.

What really happened was that these meditative-like states of mind allowed your brain to wander. I understand that you likely have been programmed to see daydreaming as a waste of time, but it's actually critical to your success. These new insights can provide evidence to your subconscious beliefs that your conscious beliefs are justified. Back to our familiar metaphor, giving your subconscious an insight is like giving your gorilla a banana. It brings a little bit of peace.

. . . .

INNERCISE: In the Clouds

An undisturbed daydreaming session, where your mind drifts in any direction it pleases, can help you let go of your limiting beliefs and allow your imagination to stretch.

1. Take a few moments to get settled in a comfortable position, close your eyes, and breathe in through your nostrils and out through your mouth. Once you are aware of your stillness within, imagine in your mind's eye that you are floating on a perfect, puffy white cloud.

2. Now as you gently float up and around on this cloud, feel how relaxing it is to be free. Notice the warm sun and gentle breeze on your face. Enjoy the weightlessness, the total feeling of letting go, and the full awareness of all of your senses.

3. Allow yourself to daydream on your drifting cloud for as long as you'd like, and when you are ready to return from the journey, drift back down to where you started, and slowly open your eyes. Take a few moments to write down your experience. What did you daydream about? Did any realizations or ideas come to the surface?

So, the next time you are on a boring group conference call or waiting for your friend to arrive or sitting on an airplane, put aside the phone/book/device and try to not think about anything. Just let your thoughts drift naturally, up into the clouds, and see what happens.

. . . .

2. Take Baby Steps

Changing your beliefs is treading in delicate territory. Being happy with your income, or increasing your income, for example, might require that you

- Change your beliefs about the meaning of money.

- Change your belief about your role at work, your job, your employer, or even your profession.

- Change your beliefs about the negative impact you think money might have.

- Change your beliefs about people who are wealthy.

- Change your belief about your ability to start a business.

- Shift your view of your own skills, abilities, and potential.

- Change the story that you tell yourself about money, wealth, and your potential.

- Change what you believe is possible for you to achieve.

These are very fundamental beliefs at the core of your self-identity. Even if you were to go in the opposite direction and denounce materialism and live off the grid, they would still shape most of your waking moments. When you try to change them, even if you don't consciously feel afraid, they can be perceived by your brain as a threat.

One way to address this is to focus on small changes. Research shows that change is interpreted by the brain as stressful. When people are asked to make a big change, fMRI studies show that the fear center in your brain can push you into fight, flight, or freeze mode.

Small changes, however, may still activate your fear response, but much less intensely, thus making them more manageable. We'll look at baby steps and creating brain friendly action plans in the upcoming Part III.

. . . .

INNERCISE: Open Window

The "Open Window" Innercise is something I have taught to thousands of students, particularly as a bridge to help them transition from having very firm limiting beliefs to more truthful ones.

Start by writing down three disempowering beliefs you have. For example,

- I'm not smart enough.
- I'm too old.
- I'm not deserving.
- I'm not skilled enough.
- Create your own: I'm_____
  _____.

Now, say them out loud and notice how they make you feel.

Next, say the sentence with a little modification. Instead of "I'm not smart enough," say, "In the past, I used to believe that I wasn't smart enough. Now I'm discovering how to be smart enough, so I can achieve my goals."

Instead of saying, "I'm too old," say, "I used to believe that I was too old to accomplish what I want. But now I understand I'm at the perfect age to take all my life's lessons and achieve my goals."

When you change the way you talk to yourself and give yourself an open window through which to learn, grow, apply, and achieve, you can activate the genius part of your brain to help guide you down a path to achieve what you choose rather than get tangled up in a list of why you can't.

The more you become aware of your automatic disempowering beliefs and self-talk that are happening beneath the surface, the more capable you become to transform this inner dialogue to that which is empowering. Whatever you believe and say to yourself reinforce neural patterns and instruct your brain on what behaviors to follow through on.

. . . .

3. Visualize and Take Action

During the time when was I struggling to change my income set point in my early real estate business, one of the powerful Innercises I used every day was visualizing in explicit detail reaching and then enjoying my new achievements.

As you'll see in Part III, visualization of your goals activates the *nucleus accumbens* and *insula,* parts of the brain that drive your motivational center and trigger your feel-good neurotransmitters.

In turn, the more you take action, the more your explicit beliefs, your outer reality, begins to align with your new, empowering, implicit beliefs. Until eventually, the new reality leads your implicit beliefs, instead of the other way around.

. . . .

INNERCISE: Back to the Future

For the next five to seven days, repeat the following new story and affirmations twice per day:

Step 1. Write a story of your future life; one where you have already achieved your most important goals and visions for your life. Include positive statements, in the present tense, such as

- I am so happy now that I have achieved…
- I am so grateful for the fact that I am now…
- It is wonderful to wake up each day knowing that…
- I am so excited now that I am able to…
- I feel so relieved now that I can…
- Finally, I am able to…
- It is amazing to experience this level of freedom and…

Feel free to use your creative license to paint your ideal life scenario in as much detail as possible. Your brain loves these specifics. As my friend Dr. David Krueger says, "First you create your story, then your story creates you."

Step 2. Sit quietly. Take five minutes and read your story as you visualize and emotionalize yourself ALREADY living the life that you just wrote about in Step 1. Go into as much detail as possible. For example,

- What are you wearing?
- Who is with you?
- What are you doing? Experiencing?

- What do you see? Smell? Hear? Taste? Sense?
- What does it feel like to have this?

On this last point, use your imagination to *feel* what it's like to truly be in this new reality. *Emotionalize* your vision.

Don't be discouraged if you can't immerse yourself in this exercise at first. It takes practice to focus your attention through spaced repetition over many days. The objective is to practice until the vision feels normal. Don't worry if you struggle to see it all clearly. Just keep trying.

Your brain is always seeking information and evidence to support your subconscious implicit beliefs, and left to its own devices, it almost always finds them. To shift your beliefs, train your brain to look for evidence that supports the new beliefs you're trying to create in the brain.

As an example, one of our Winning the Game of Money clients wrote the following "Money Story" for herself. She reads, emotionalizes, and visualizes it daily to activate the motivational center and the left prefrontal cortex of her brain:

- I'm so happy and grateful for the fact that I have so much to offer to the world. I belong, and I contribute every day.

- I now have all the knowledge and skills to understand and release the patterns that have held me back in the past, and I'm doing that daily.

- I find ways to invest more time on moneymaking activities, and I'm doing this each day. Using my skills to earn money is hugely enjoyable.

- I fully believe that I am now deserving and worthy of belonging in the flow of money. I am one with money and money is one with me.

- I am able to overcome any obstacles that come my way. I feel confident that I can live a fulfilling life that respects my natural introverted propensities.

- I am willing and able to leave behind my fears of putting myself out there, in front of people. My knowledge is extensive, and I deserve to be listened to.

- I am willing to do whatever it takes to earn money that suits my soul. Everything I do is aligned with my spiritual purpose and brings me the freedom I seek.

- I am now ready to align my thoughts, emotions, and behaviors with my soul. My purpose is to spread unconditional love, and everything I do is a reflection of that.

- I am good enough. My heart is pure, and my new reality is a projection of my heart.

- The feelings that I now have around my money story are powerful. They support me with more confidence, clarity, and energy.

- It feels amazing to believe in my abilities and my future fully. I am so grateful to John and the community for supporting me.

- Even though at times I feel uncomfortable, I am certain of my progress and growth. I am doing what it takes to move my life forward.

- I am doing the things daily that are giving me the highest joy. I am aligned spiritually, mentally, and emotionally, and I am a giver of love. It feels amazing.

· ·

Innercise: Exhibit A

This Innercise is designed to help you intentionally find evidence to support new, empowering beliefs, instead of disempowering ones.

1. What is the most limiting belief about yourself that you can identify?

2. On an index card, write the *opposite* of that belief, or a modified version.

   For example,

   If you have a belief that, "Rich people are greedy," you might write a statement such as "Some rich people are generous."

   If you believe, "I'm not smart enough to be rich," you might write, "I am smart enough to be as rich as I choose. I do smart things every day."

3. Carry this card with you every day and *look for evidence to support your new belief.* When you find it, write it on the back of the card.

Change Your Story, Change Your Life

Dr. David Krueger, an exceptional retired psychiatrist and NeuroGym collaborator, is the father of a seven-step strategy for reshaping any disempowering mental story. Here's how it works:

- **Recognize Authorship.** Anyone who's serious about improving their life must recognize that they're the authors of their story. These stories create a framework of possibilities, good or bad. Without first recognizing that you're the author of your own story, there's virtually no path forward for improvement.

- **Be Accountable.** With awareness of authorship, comes accountability. You have to own your story if you're serious about making changes to it.

- **Assess Your Story.** You have to discover what your story is made up of. What's the plot and the story line? Who are the characters? What recurring patterns and results keep showing up? Looking at it objectively in this way will help you reshape it.

- **Decide What to Change.** Figure out which parts of your story you need to let go of and which you need to keep.

- **Map Your Changes.** To alter your story, you need a road map to get you to where you want

- to end up. So, itemize new goals and strategies to take you from here to there.

- **Start Authoring New Experiences**. Author your new life story by creating affirmations, visualizations, and real-life experiences that validate your new story line and plot. Considering that much of your behavior is steeped in habits, repetitive brain retraining, including emotionalizing these new experiences, is essential.

- **Program a New Identity.** Along with creating a new life story, it is crucial that you also create a sense of self-image that can sustain your new explicit and implicit alignments.

You deserve a lot of recognition for your courage, fortitude, and integrity to first uncover your subconscious story, and then to consciously rewrite it.

Self-Image: The Most Important Belief of All

Everyone has two images of themselves—the one they want to believe, and the hidden one they *really* believe.

When it comes to achieving financial, physical, relational, spiritual, or other goals, if your subconscious beliefs about yourself don't match your conscious goals, the result is almost always neural dissonance. In essence, your "in" doesn't match your "out" and your "in" most likely will win that battle.

This makes what you think and feel about *yourself* most important in your life. So, when you change your beliefs, any beliefs, you also challenge the *story you tell about yourself*. It's a story with many parts that touch all aspects of your life. A real gut check happens then when you *start telling yourself new stories*, better stories, more self-compassionate stories about yourself. Changing your self-image is not for the faint of heart as your very existence is called into question. For instance,

- Do you tell yourself a story of how you're helplessly addicted to food? Or do you tell a story of working to change your eating habits and lifestyle?

- Do you spin a tale in your mind that you're a nine-to-fiver and not smart enough to start a business? Or do you weave one of researching new opportunities and learning entrepreneurial skills?

- Do you tell yourself that you need money to make money? Or do you tell a story of creative financing available to so many people from all backgrounds?

These are all examples of shifting your beliefs about yourself and your worldview, but they also share a crucial common thread. Whereas the first stories are about permanence and powerlessness, the alternative stories are about potential and empowerment.

Building a healthy self-image is essential for change, and because the only thing that's certain is that change will continue to happen, maintaining a healthy self-image will remain essential for your entire change in order to live to your fullest. You can help yourself stay on top of this responsibility by carefully and consciously taking steps forward. Answer the following questions to help you with those steps:

- Do you have a clear, written vision for what you want your life to be?

- Have you identified the limiting beliefs that may be holding you back?

- Are you working to replace those beliefs with supportive ones?

- Have you upgraded your knowledge and skills to build your confidence?

- Are you taking small action steps to build more self-trust and confidence?

This belief that change is possible has its home in the brain too. Researchers divide the core principles behind this possibility into two types—*fixed* and *growth* mindsets. Those with the former mindset believe that their basic abilities, talents, and intelligence are fixed traits. You get what you get and do the best you can with it. Those with the latter mindset, however, believe their abilities, talents, and intelligence can be improved upon. They believe that by trying and continuing to work at it, they can grow.

For example, a fixed mindset statement would be "I'm not good with money." While a growth mindset statement would be "I'm going to learn to get better with money."

There's leading-edge research backing this understanding too. When researchers look at brain activity in people with growth versus fixed mindsets, they find that those with growth mindsets experience more brain activity *when they make a mistake.*[21] They are, the researchers have concluded, more aware of their mistakes. And as we know, awareness is critical. Once you're aware of a mistake, you can take action to avoid repeating it in the future. Thus, you can change. You are not strictly confined to the hand that was dealt you.

This is incredibly important because change of *any* kind is filled with mistakes. As they say, you can't make an omelet without breaking a few eggs, and as you begin to shift your beliefs and make changes in your life, you're going to break more than your share. The question then is *Will you be aware of your mistakes, and therefore learn from them and change? Or* will you continue to make the same mistakes, possibly even give up on changing?

What this all means is that shifting your beliefs is fundamentally about adopting a growth mindset.

In order to grow, you have to believe you can.

Real People. Real Results.

Heidi is fifty-three, a licensed Marriage and Family Therapist, happily married, has two successful adult children and lots of friends, and was thoroughly enjoying her life in all but one area. She couldn't understand how being a mother, wife, friend, therapist, etc., came so easily while her body was desperately suffering. "I was 55 lbs. overweight, riddled with Crohn's disease, in constant pain, and feeling completely hopeless."

Heidi recalls compulsively overeating throughout her childhood and being praised for her body's ability to eat large amounts of food without consequence. "You're an athlete! Your body needs it!" she was constantly told. She experienced tremendous joy around food.

She recalls the first time her husband witnessed her binge. "He appeared shocked and deeply concerned," she said. She never really recognized it as problematic behavior until that moment when her husband said, "Wow, do you really want to eat that much food?" She didn't know how to respond because that is all she had ever known. Feeling shameful and embarrassed, she decided in that moment to only binge in private. Lots of secrecy, dishonesty, and negative energy manifested with that decision.

She spent the next twenty plus years trying different diet programs that helped her lose weight at first, but eventually she gained it all back and then some. She developed Crohn's disease and took countless medications and injections that helped for a short time but were not a long-term solution. "There just has to be a better way," she prayed.

While searching the Internet, she discovered John Assaraf and MyNeurogym.com. Heidi started to Innercise and retrain her subconscious mind and reset her health mindset and "fat set" point using the Winning the Game of Weight Loss program. It gave her the ability to better control her emotions and behavior around food. "I walk 2.5 miles around my neighborhood loop and listen to the audio Innercises two or three times and all within sixty minutes! I LOVE IT!" She started feeling and seeing things shift pretty quickly. "I KNEW intuitively I was exactly where I needed to be. I released and have kept off over 55 lbs and my Crohn's disease is gone! I am so happy, hopeful, and my confidence is growing daily."

Heidi and her husband Dave have never been better and her adult children now understand their health and well-being are completely in their hands. She is so excited with her journey back to health and happiness.

Chapter Summary and Resources

Summary

- Beliefs help drive your behavior and form your reality.

- The conscious/subconscious divide in your brain creates two types of beliefs: *explicit—ones you are conscious of;* and *implicit—ones hidden in your subconscious.*

- When you try to change, your explicit and implicit beliefs don't align and you'll likely experience cognitive dissonance, which will result in your implicit beliefs trying to bring things back to the status quo, including by self-harming and self-sabotaging.

- Many of your implicit beliefs that don't serve you well can be identified and changed.

Additional Free Resources

If you want additional help and free resources on how to best use each section in the book, I'm including some special coaching videos and 9 mini brain-training audios to go along with the book. I will act as your mindset coach as part of buying Innercise. For now, get started with this book and the free resources. Just scan the code below on your smartphone and log in to the NeuroGym platform or go to www.myneurogym.com/innercise to create a log in so you gain access to the free bonuses and resources.

Stress and Anxiety

From Suffering to Surfing

"The greatest weapon against stress is our ability to choose one thought over another."

—William James

Pe'ahi, or more commonly known by its nickname, "Jaws," is the legendary reef break off Maui. Depending on your outlook, riding its 60-foot waves is nirvana if you're Laird Hamilton and other tow-in surfers who say it feels like touching the face of God. Rumor has it Jaws can churn out monstrous 120 footers.

On the other side of the planet on November 8, 2017, at Nazaré, Portugal, Rodrigo Koxa set the current world record barreling down an 80-foot wave: "I have tried to surf big waves all my life and I had a huge experience in 2014 where I almost died at Nazaré. Four months later, I still had bad dreams. I didn't travel, I got scared, and my wife helped me psychologically. Now, I'm just so happy and this is the best day of my life. It's a dream come true."

Huge waves have long been used as metaphors to describe mounting stress—a climbing, powerful, unstoppable force that then smashes us onto the rocks. But while stress can wash us ashore in a heap, it can also be harnessed to give us performance we never imagined.

Stress as Strength

Typically, stress is seen as something that happens when we feel that the demands placed on us are greater than our ability to handle them. Stress then is a perceived imbalance between needs and available resources. For example, if you feel like you have more work on your desk than you have time to do it, or you have a task that's beyond your passion or skill level, you likely become stressed. And if your bills exceed the money you have, the same.

In the summer of 1936, Hans Selye, a Hungarian researcher, published a paper in the science journal *Nature* that described what he called "noxious agents" in writing about how the body deals with stress. He explained that there's a universal response common to all people. First there's an "alarm reaction" followed by a "fight or flight" reaction. There's a lot more to Selye's research, most notably that it set into motion a whole new field of study on the biological effects of stress: the general consensus being that stress was *bad*. Being overwhelmed, overworked, and in too deep was bad for our health, jobs, and relationships. Stress was something to be avoided at all costs.

This thinking though couldn't effectively address how some people, when faced with a typical wave of stress, actually seemed to function better. In fact, they didn't just seem to do better, they visibly *thrived*. As researchers continued these studies, lo and behold, they found some stress is really good for you.

In this chapter, you'll learn how you can take stress, and its close cousin *anxiety*, and use Innercises to manage them and turn them to your advantage.

Surfing vs. Suffering: The Two Types of Stress Response

Give some people a wave and they'll wash up on the rocks. They *suffer*. Give the same wave to someone else and they'll ride it for the best time of their life. They *surf*.

These two responses are so distinct that stress researchers have given them names. When we experience stress as an overwhelming force we can't handle, it's called a *threat response*. Conversely, when we experience stress as a source of energy and initiative, it's called a *challenge* response.

These two are more than just labels—our brains and bodies actually behave differently in each case. The threat response is fundamentally a fear response. When you perceive stress as more than you can handle, your body sends you into fight, flight, freeze, or faint mode. You tighten, constrict, and prepare for survival. You narrow your focus.

With the challenge response, your body relaxes, your breath steadies, and you go with the flow. You broaden your focus.

Threat Response (Suffer and survive)	Challenge Response (Surf and thrive)
Fight, flight, freeze, or faint	Relax/respond
Erratic, higher heartbeat	Lower heartbeat
Narrow focus	Calm focus
Reactive	Creative
Fear, helplessness, despair, anxiety	Inspiration, courage, pride
Tight muscles, shallow or held breath	Loose muscles, steady breath
Constricted blood vessels, blood flow	Relaxed blood vessels, blood flow

Just by looking at the list above, it's easy to see how dramatically your results can differ depending on your response. For example, faced with a crushing workload and deadline, a threat response might be to

- "Choke" and drop the ball at a key sales presentation.

- Lash out in anger at a coworker or family member.

- Retreat to calling in sick, downing a quart of Ben & Jerry's Chunky Monkey ice cream, or binge-watching all four seasons of your favorite show.

- Develop tunnel vision and struggle to think clearly.

A challenge response, on the other hand, might be to

- Increase your productivity and make fewer mistakes.

- Find a calm flow of energy to work alone or with others.

- Relax, breathe deeply, and calm yourself.

- Broaden your vision and develop a variety of ideas to choose from.

In each case the stressor is the same; it's the *response* that is different.

Admittedly, the first response is the one you likely encounter more frequently. It's your ancient brain meeting today's world, and it's a recipe for stress.

The first lesson from this then is that *it's not the stressor itself, but how you process and respond to it that determines your outcomes.*

The second lesson is that your responses tend to be habitual—and that's something you can change.

What's Your Stress Habit?

Let's go back to what might seem like that Hawaiian 60-foot Pe'ahi wave bearing down on you. Perhaps the wave is a crisis at work—one more thing on your overwhelming to-do list. But it's not just another fire to put out, it's an earth-scorcher.

So, you're essentially faced with two choices. The first is to allow the fear response of your ancient brain to take control, pushing you into classic fight, flight, or freeze mode. Technically, you could faint too, but I'm guessing you'll keep awake. Here is what the results will look like:

Fight: You might push back or lash out, making the situation worse.

Flight: You might conveniently have appointments outside the office in an attempt to escape or avoid the situation. That won't stop the wave from coming, but maybe it'll buy you time to get your head together, or maybe you'll get lucky and the problem will work itself out without you.

Freeze: You check your emails for the hundredth time waiting for an answer from someone. From anyone, because you know you don't have any.

This is your *default stress response.* It's a habit—a pattern of thinking that kicks in at the first sign of trouble. It's the gorilla pounding his chest.

If you have a tendency toward a threat response to stress, then your first job is to learn how to interrupt this default mode so that you can alternatively choose a challenge response.

. . . .

INNERCISE: Surf the Wave

If you're feeling overwhelmed, you can learn to take control of your stress response using the following steps based on the work of my good friend, Dr. Daniel Friedland, MD:

1. *Pause.* Allow yourself to notice whatever you're feeling without judgment or resistance.

2. *Take six slow breaths.* The breathing will help to keep you from slipping into a threat response. (See the "Take 6" Innercise.)

3. *Observe your body, thoughts, and feelings.* Note: without judgment, or any physical, emotional, or mental stress.

4. *Name what you're experiencing.* For example, "anger" or "irritation" or "overwhelm." If you're overwhelmed, just silently and kindly say, "I feel overwhelmed…I choose to release it." If you're irritated, just silently and kindly say, "I am upset…I choose to release it."

Using this simple Innercise, you can consciously gain more control of your subconscious reactions and calm yourself. Once you do that, you can then change your response. Just doing this Innercise changes your brain. Rather than being swept away by the current of emotions, you can ride the wave.

. . . .

Anxiety: Learning to Deal with Chronic Worry

Anxiety is closely related to stress. Think of it as the forward-thinking cousin of stress. Whereas stress is a perceived imbalance of demands and resources, anxiety is essentially *worrying* about that imbalance.

For instance, when you go into threat mode at your job after another problem lands on your desk, that's stress. When you can't sleep at night because you're obsessing over whether you'll be able to handle the problem, that's anxiety.

As with stress, however, you can actively hack into parts of the system that contribute to anxiety and slow down your mind.

Monkey Mind

Monkey mind. It sounds funny, I know. But it's a real term from Buddhism that refers to how, when left unoccupied, our minds have a tendency to become restless, indecisive, and preoccupied—like a troop of monkeys swinging wildly from tree to tree, chattering, screeching, flinging feces, and generally raising all manners of hell.

You've undoubtedly felt the monkey mind at work in your own life. In the jungle of your mind, your restful, and restless, brain can run amok with all sorts of monkey business. Too much time spent imagining future problems, rehashing old ones, and worrying endlessly about "what-ifs" that are likely to never happen often lead to a long list of headaches we're all familiar with: anxiety, thinking in circles, negative self-talk, indecisiveness, sleeplessness, and even depression.

While the expression "monkey mind" might have been coined by the Buddha more than two thousand years ago, two things make it as relevant today as ever. First, our attention is becoming increasingly fragmented, meaning that the monkeys are more active than ever. Second, science is beginning to understand at a neurological level what monkey mind looks like. Both of these factors help give us some insight into how to better manage this mayhem.

Meet Your Troop of Neuro-Monkeys

When your mind is relaxed, it doesn't just go to sleep. It's still active. In fact, there are many areas of a calm mind that actually become more active. Those include brain regions like the *medial prefrontal cortex, hippocampus, medial parietal cortex, medial temporal lobes, and the posterior cingulate cortex.*[22]

Researchers sometimes group these areas into a system called the Default Mode Network (DMN). For example, when you're not actively focused on a task but instead are day-dreaming, the DMN becomes *more* active. And as we know, letting the mind wander is essential for creativity, relaxation, and perspective. Other research shows it can help your brain assimilate and organize new information you learn.

So, a few monkeys are a good thing. But as is so often the case, too much of a good thing can become a problem. Which means too much DMN can lead to monkey mind and you might find yourself becoming immobilized by negative self-talk and indecision.

But here comes Innercise to the rescue to help you manage activity in your noisy prefrontal lobes and flex your core neuro-muscles supporting awareness. The Innercise tools of choice are mindfulness and meditation—especially to focus on those prefrontal lobes where much of the chatter lives.

It's remarkable to think that just ten years ago or so, meditation and mindfulness were still out in the cold fringes of society. But today they are fully embraced by the mainstream. Harvard Business School teaches its MBAs the value of mindfulness for increasing profits, managing labor disputes, scaling to higher levels of operational performance, and more. Look into Google, Aetna, General Mills, and Goldman Sachs and you'll find mindfulness and meditation to be common business practices—as common as R&D and sales trainings. The best medical centers in the world—Massachusetts General Hospital (Boston), Johns Hopkins Hospital (Baltimore), Mayo Clinic (Rochester, Minnesota)—have all incorporated mindfulness and mediation into their wellness programs. These practices benefited patients by reducing the incidence of illness and speeding recovery times for those afflicted.

To be clear, meditation is not as passive as it looks. You don't just sit there in the lotus position. You actively train your mind to increase your awareness.

But you also don't need to be a monk to enjoy the benefits. Researchers have found that even modest amounts of meditation practice can change the brain,[23] quiet the DMN,[24] and increase your gray matter[25] especially in the areas that involve learning, emotional regulation, and perspective.

. . . .

INNERCISE: Meditation

This simple meditation practice only takes five to seven minutes to complete. You can do it anywhere, anytime.

First, find a place to sit quietly and comfortably. Next, do the "TAKE 6: Calm the Circuits" Innercise.

"TAKE 6: Calm the Circuits"

Take six deep rhythmic breaths in through your nose and out through your mouth, like you are blowing out of a straw. As you breathe in, say,

I breathe in calmness, I breathe out stress.
or
I breathe in calmness, I breathe out fear.
or
I breathe in calmness, I breathe out anxiety, or overwhelm.

Next, do the AiA Innercise and become aware of your thoughts, emotions, feelings, and sensations without judgment—just revel in pure awareness; smile as you become aware of how good this feels.

AiA INNERCISE

In a calm relaxed frame of mind (as you gently breathe in and out) be aware of your physiology, your mental and emotional state, and the behavior you are engaged in. (Awareness)

Next ask yourself "What is my intention for this moment?" Is it to be angry? Sad? Mad or frustrated, or to be calm and able to respond instead of react? (Intention)

Once you choose your intention and direction, take one small, simple action-step toward achieving your goal. (Action)

AWARENESS INNERCISE

Deliberately focus your attention on the toes of your left foot and move them around. Go slowly up the left side of your body and stop wherever you like. Be aware of that body part, and then move on, all the way up your left side and down the right.

Notice your physical body. Be aware of how you are sitting, breathing, and feeling.

Do this for five minutes in a totally calm and relaxed state. Release any expectations or judgment. Just deliberately direct your attention.

Self-awareness is the first key to change and doing this basic meditation will go a long way in building your ability to direct your focus and attention.

....

The Daydreaming Sweet Spot

Like so many things in the brain, there's a sweet spot for creating a balance between your prefrontal cortex and your DMN—somewhere between being overrun by monkeys and healthy daydreaming. That epiphany you had in the shower? That's your sweet spot.

When you move between daydreaming and paying attention you use a part of your brain called the insula. The *insula* acts as a kind of switch to help you move from one state to the other. So, when you move from your DMN to your more conscious, deliberate brain functions, the insula facilitates that transition.[26] For example, when you're daydreaming (or worrying anxiously) and your phone rings, it is your insula that brings you back to the present so you can respond to the incoming call.

Think of meditation and mindfulness as friends to your insula. They can help you actively cultivate those shifts from one state to another, without having to wait for a phone to ring or another disruption that will snap you awake. That means when the monkeys are running loose, there are some conscious choices you can make to settle them down. One of my favorites is a powerful Innercise that helps reset and quiet your mind.

Stress Inoculation: Changing Your Relationship with Stress and Anxiety

Odds are that there have been times when you've still felt tired even after a long sleep and felt like you can't seem to finish things even though you've been working hard at it. This may be a sign of having an ongoing threat response to stress.

Your brain isn't designed for long-term stress. Stress hormones such as cortisol are like rocket fuel, so a constant threat response can end up draining you. For instance, you might begin to feel like easy things—stuff you can usually handle effortlessly, say answering routine emails—become difficult. And in time, the difficult might begin to feel impossible.

Too much stress also damages your memory and your immune system. It can inhibit your executive functions and motor skills to a degree that you not only reduce your ability to perform at your highest level but you can also eventually burn out—that's lights out; you're fried.

Preventing this requires two basic behaviors. The first is to *give yourself breaks between waves.* This means more than just going away on vacations. While those are helpful, your brain requires more downtime to reset than just those special occasions each year.

I use the following Innercise to create specific reset times throughout my day, every day. It's fast and it increases both my sense of greater control and greater productivity.

. . . .

INNERCISE: Adult Chill Out Time

- Choose three times in the day when you can schedule your *own personal time* for just three to five minutes.

- Set your phone, computer, or watch, or ask someone you trust, to gently remind you of your scheduled time.

- At the scheduled time, *stop what you're doing and take a few relaxing breaths.*

- When your mind begins to clear, step away from your immediate environment and stretch or walk for just a moment or two. Look out the window, or otherwise disengage your senses from what you had been focused on.

That's it! Wrap up your time out and then get back to the task at hand. You'll likely find you can get more done in less time and feel more in control of your life.

Tips:

- For this Innercise to work best, *you need to schedule these in three- to five-minute resets.* Putting them in a calendar works well for most people.

- Start with three times a day for a week, and then increase to four to six times a day. Experiment to see what schedule works best for you. Perhaps it's every hour in the morning, and a few more times in the afternoon and evening.

. . . .

The second important behavior for avoiding burnout is to change your relationship with stress.

Research shows that how you feel about stress itself can play a large role in how you respond to it. For example, if you feel stress is a negative force in your life—that every wave is a crushing, dangerous defeat, then you're more likely to experience it that way and have the expected results.[27]

But before you start stressing over how this sounds like you and how you should be doing better, this might help you put things in perspective: It is a common belief in our culture that *all* stress is negative. While we know there are positives to healthy levels of stress, there is far more literature, both from scientific studies and studies adapted for the layperson, that reveals the harmful consequences of stress and advocating stress management. And according to the U.S. Centers for Disease Control and Prevention, "Stress is a factor in five out of the six leading causes of death—heart disease, cancer, stroke, lower respiratory disease, and accidents." And the National Institutes of Health reports, "An estimated 75 percent to 90 percent of all doctor visits are for stress-related issues." In the face of these heavyweights, it's no wonder squeezing in a word about the positive side of some stress doesn't get much airplay. But it's true: perception of a negative stress can be changed to a perception of positivity. For example, when you feel stressed about your work, or your relationships, or your health—it's because they matter to you. So instead of seeing stress as a threat, reframe it: Think of it as a sign of *something you care about; something you can embrace to* give new meaning to your life. Degree of adeptness at this reframing is a large reason why some people flourish and others flounder under equal amounts of stress.

If you find yourself avoiding all stress in your life, or constantly feeling harmful effects from stress, consider asking yourself these questions as a way to help you improve your reframing abilities:

- Are the things I'm avoiding truly stressful or dangerous, or do I just need to improve my skills?

- Might other people reasonably see my situation as a meaningful challenge, or as an opportunity for growth? How and why might they see it that way?

- Do I know of anyone facing similar challenges who seems to be moving forward instead of being stuck? Why might that be?

From Monkeys to Monks

Most are truly unaware of their low-level chronic stress and anxiety. And because they're not aware of it, they don't realize there are steps they could take to improve their stress response. From this chronic state, even though it's at a lower level, just a moment of overwhelm can be enough for the fear center of your brain to hijack your operations and you end up spending your day consumed in fight/flight/freeze mode.

A good place to start then is using your awareness neuro-muscles to recognize stress and anxiety as they arise. With Innercise, you can do that, and reach a state where you can take more deliberate control of your lower-level chronic conditions as well as your higher-level overwhelms. With enough practice, you can be more like a monk instead of a monkey: calm, aware, and better able to choose your thoughts, feelings, and behaviors.

Real mastery of stress can come when you first notice the wave building and then effectively calm yourself in that moment. Those are the times when you can truly move from the fear centers of your brain to your executive function centers. Those are pivotal times when you *choose* and *use* the best practices for living to your fullest potential.

. . . .

INNERCISE: Pain, Pain, Go Away

This Innercise uses negative consequences to start off with but will turn into positive ones very shortly. Stop whatever you are doing and focus on these words:

> If you do not release the disempowering thoughts, emotions, habits, and behaviors that are keeping you stuck right now, who other than you will suffer? How? Will it be your children? Your spouse? Your colleagues?

Next, play a mental movie in your mind and see the people in your life who will be negatively affected if you stick to your current beliefs, habits, stories, or excuses. How does this make you feel? What are the thoughts you are having about yourself right now and about them?

Go as deep as you can into these questions, diving into what your life would be like knowing that you have it in your power to change but you choose not to. You have it in your power to make a bigger difference, but you don't. Why? How do you believe those negatively affected by your choices are feeling as a result?

Now, as you finish this part of the Innercise, start anew with Innercise: Take 6 Calm the Circuits.

. . . .

"TAKE 6: Calm the Circuits"

Take six deep rhythmic breaths in through your nose and out through your mouth, like you are blowing out of a straw. As you breathe in, say,

I breathe in calmness, I breathe out stress.
or
I breathe in calmness, I breathe out fear.
or
I breathe in calmness, I breathe out anxiety, or overwhelm.

As you continue to take gentle breaths in through your nose and out through your mouth, see and feel what your life will be like when you choose to change and take the actions needed to make it the masterpiece it is meant to be.

See and feel the lives of those you love and those who you will impact in a positive way as a result of strengthening your mindset and upgrading your emotional skills.

Feel their emotions and gratitude. Feel how proud you are of yourself, knowing you took control and you took action today—how else does this make you feel? Keep these feelings going as you play the mental movie in your mind; then add a little tapping on your temples with both of your hands and fingers. Anchor the mental movie with your tapping and deep emotions and smile with joy for your gratitude and love for yourself.

This Innercise uses activation of the stress circuits as a way to create contrast between what change could bring versus what staying the same could bring. The conclusion: Change and empower yourself with Innercise.

Real People. Real Results.

George Carroll was a proud father of two young boys.

After finding himself in heavy amounts of debt, he realized that if he continued down the path he was one, he wasn't going to be able to give his children the kind of life they deserved. The thing is, George suffered from some negative mental programming—something he didn't realize until things got bad.

George explains: "By the time I left college at twenty-three, I had $25,000 in debt from student loans and credit cards. I had a lot of bad habits with money and I basically just repeated the same patterns over and over the course of time until eventually…I went bankrupt."

George was a hard worker though. And he did whatever he could to try and build a better life. But something still stood in his way: "It took a while, but I started to dig myself out of my hole, rebuild my life, and raise my income. But as soon as I passed the $100,000 mark, I would unconsciously self-sabotage."

That's when he told himself, "I got to take a really hard look at what's going on in my brain with money."

George started Innercising daily and pretty soon, his life started to change. "If I would have never found NeuroGym, I think I would still be hitting that same income ceiling over and over. Innercising helped me change my subconscious programming so that it's now aligned with my goals. I no longer see or feel that ceiling. Since I've started, my seminar business has doubled each of the last two years."

George realized that the greatest resource we all have is time. For most of his life, he let his bad habits and destructive subconscious programming about money take control of his thoughts and actions. But once he committed to Innercising he was finally able to create a better life for his family. A life that gave him the freedom to spend time with the people he loved most.

Chapter Summary and Resources

Summary

- Stress can be experienced as a wave that crushes you or one that you surf to the shores of success.

- Your response to stress, not the stress-inducing event itself, determines your feelings and emotions.

- Chronic worry and anxiety can be replaced with sustained quiet and happiness through Innercises such as meditation and mindfulness.

- Real mastery of stress can come when you first notice the wave building and then you effectively calm yourself in that moment.

- Think of stress not as bad, but rather as a sign of something you care about and something you can grow from.

Additional Free Resources

If you want additional help and free resources on how to best use each section in the book, I'm including some special coaching videos and 9 mini brain-training audios to go along with the book. I will act as your mindset coach as part of buying Innercise. For now, get started with this book and the free resources. Just scan the code below on your smartphone and log in to the NeuroGym platform or go to www.myneurogym.com/innercise to create a log in so you gain access to the free bonuses and resources.

Mindset

From Negativity to Positivity

"Ninety percent of your long-term happiness is predicted not by the external world, but by the way your brain processes the world."

—Shawn Achor, author and happiness researcher

Legend has it that an angry young man once sought advice from his grandfather, a wise elder in his tribe. The young man had been wronged by another tribesman and struggled with his desire for revenge. Sitting on the ground across the fire from his elder, he opened:

"Each night I'm filled with thoughts of anger. I imagine taking revenge in horrible ways. I wish ill will toward my brother. By day, I'm unhappy. My wounds fester in me, and I can think of nothing else. I know this is wrong, but I can't seem to stop."

As was his way, the grandfather sat in silence before he spoke. At last, "I too struggled with this. I will tell you what my grandfather told me when I was your age. He said that within each of us lives two wolves. One is dark. It is the worst of us—anger, jealousy, fear, sorrow, regret, pride, insecurity, self-pity, and resentment. But there is also a light wolf within us. He is us at our best—generous, grateful, loving, kind, hopeful, compassionate, and humble. Both wolves are strong. And they battle constantly for dominance within us. Each wanting control, each wanting to enslave the other."

The young man listened—his grandfather had described exactly how he felt.

"Tell me Grandfather," he said. "I feel like a crazy man. I must know. Which wolf wins?"

The elder looked up from the fire for the first time and stared into the young man's eyes.

"The one who wins," he said softly, "is the one you constantly *feed.*"

This story has been repeated many times, in many forms, and attributed to many sources, but the lesson is the same across all versions: *Focus on the positive.*

There's a reason for this. A positive mindset—a term we'll use broadly here to encompass an attitude of optimism, happiness, and creativity—has been shown time and again to be tied to success. Regardless of your situation, feeding your optimism, happiness, and creativity is a critical part of your path forward. While feeding pessimism, suffering, and closed-mindedness will inevitably hold you back.

I'm sure you already know building and then holding onto this positive mindset is a lot *easier said than done.* In times of stress, fear, anxiety, and uncertainty, negativity can seem as if it comes hardwired into our operating system. And I'm sure you already know that there is a time and place where being negative can be a lifesaver—more on this in a moment.

Why We're So Positively Negative

Why did I even open my mouth? This will never work. Beggars can't be choosers.

That little voice—the dark wolf, if we go by the legend above—is a challenge for each of us. We all have at times insisted on seeing more potential problems than potential opportunities in a generally good situation.

But why?

Our Negativity Bias

Here's a thought exercise for you. Imagine I hand you a needle and ask you to stick it in your body any place where it *won't* hurt. *Hmmm. There really aren't any places it won't hurt you,* right? Your entire body is covered in nerves that are very good at delivering sensory signals to your brain. And there is virtually no place on the outside of your body, other than nails and hair, where you don't feel pain. Which, by a simple calculation, means there are lots of areas where you can feel pleasure.

That enormous imbalance between pain and pleasure sensitivity in your outer body reflects a similar mismatch in your entire life. At a conscious level, you are far more attuned to pain than you are to pleasure. That's physical and emotional pain. And not just *actual* pain, but also imagined, remembered, or perceived pain.

This is no accident. As your brain evolved, a healthy dose of skepticism turned out to be a good thing. In the dangerous world of early human evolution, being more negative was a lifesaver. Being overly optimistic might have gotten you a meal or a mate, but it might have also gotten you killed: *This young antelope is good eating.* But for a stalking lion ready to pounce on both the hominid and the antelope, well…

The result of this negativity bias is our present-day brain with some predispositions. For example,

- Most people remember pain much more than they do pleasure.

- We recognize angry faces faster than happy ones.

- About two-thirds of the neurons in the amygdala—the part of the brain responsible for survival instincts, memory, emotions, and sex drive, among other functions—watch out for threats.

As neuropsychologist Dr. Rick Hanson says, "The brain is like Velcro for negative experiences but Teflon for positive ones."[28]

Those negative experiences, from your childhood through today, are locked away ready for lightning-quick referencing to keep you—according to what your brain perceives—safe. So that time you embarrassed yourself. That time you lost money in the stock market. That time you stayed in a bad relationship. That's right, those experiences are all on file for your brain to access in an attempt to protect you from getting into more danger, even if that danger is more imaginary than real.

This protectiveness, which often becomes overprotectiveness that holds you back, can reveal itself in ways you've likely never even thought of. For instance, when you

- Focus on the downside, more than the upside. As behavioral economists have shown us, we hate to lose more than we love to win.

- Overestimate risk.

- Recall that one time things went wrong, and not the hundred times things went great. Or the one criticism and not the hundred compliments.

In essence, we tend to see through smoke-colored glasses instead of rose-colored ones.

Yet, we also have 20/20 vision at times:

- The times where we feel like a ray of optimism in a room full of fear and doom

- The times when we come up with a brilliant solution to a problem that's been plaguing us

- The times when we forge ahead fearlessly into something that others would never do

- The times when we flow with creativity

These sparks of happiness, hope, and imagination can unleash a powerful *positivity* bias, and our genius within.

Einstein vs. Frankenstein: The Two "Wolves" in Your Brain

If you were to slap your forehead in a cartoon-like expression of *Duh!* you'd have placed your hand directly over your *prefrontal cortex* (PFC).

The PFC has a robust resume. It helps you plan and strategize, concentrate and learn. It helps you predict and decide. And it has a large role in determining your overall personality. It's also considered your home for good judgment—when you're so hungry that you want to grab chips or cookies or whatever is in front of you, your PFC steps in and helps you delay gratification.

Your PFC is divided nicely down the middle into two halves—left and right. And just as the PFC does a different job than the rest of the brain, its two halves in turn tend to shoulder different responsibilities too. In fact, these two halves can be so different and lead to such different behaviors, that we've given them the Innercise nicknames, Einstein and Frankenstein.

The left side of your PFC is your "inner Einstein." You might think of it as the CEO of your brain, or the orchestra conductor leading your brain in a complex symphony. It's the forward-looking, creative rock star side of you that can find elegant solutions, that can fill you with the promise of what *is* possible. When we feel motivated and at our best is when our Einstein brain is most active.

Over on the right side of your PFC, however, is your "inner Frankenstein." The dark wolf. It tends toward the promise of what *is not* possible. It focuses on constraints, barriers, and complications. Frankenstein will always look—and usually find—evidence for why something is impossible or risky. Or too threatening to the familiar status quo, even if the status quo is crying out for change. It loves to dredge up your past, but it also finds information from your present and the world you live in to be just as lovable for keeping you "safe"—that is through its perception of what is safe. While these are sometimes necessary and valuable traits for survival, too much Frankenstein often creates its own monster.

Because you have an innate negativity bias and pay more attention to potential risks, Frankenstein can keep you stuck. For many people, it is the dominant brain mode—one that often creates a mindset of pessimism, immobilization, and limitations, thus making it far more likely to be constrained by *what is,* rather than what *could be.* This means a dominant Frankenstein mode is both a cause and a perpetuator of a negative attitude.

Fortunately, Innercise is a key to striking the right balance between your Einstein and Frankenstein brains!

Your Inner Einstein	Your Inner Frankenstein
The CEO, orchestra conductor	The Doubting Debbie, Downer Dennis
Figures out solutions	Locks on to barriers
Motivator	Inhibitor
How you can	How/Why you can't
Rational optimism	Blind pessimism
Options	Constraints

Activating Your Inner Einstein with Innercise

To activate your inner Einstein while reducing the impact of your inner Frankenstein, we can rely on an important characteristic of your brain: its limited supply of resources. Even though it uses a large amount of your daily energy relative to its size, it still has to run a lean operation. This means that oftentimes when some brain processes are active, others are less active.

A perfect example of this is the fear response. When you go into fight, flight, freeze, or faint mode in response to a threat, activity in less immediately critical areas of your brain is reduced—basically it's called upon to respond to the distress signal your fear response is sending out. This is the way your brain manages energy most important for your survival. After all, there's no need for complex or abstract thinking in your left prefrontal cortex when you're running for your life.

You can use this resource management system to your advantage. Let me explain: by Innercising to activate your left PFC, you can, by default, reduce activity in the right PFC. Or, if you prefer, maximizing Einstein, by default, minimizes Frankenstein.

Four Innercises for Activating Your Inner Einstein

As with so many matters involving your brain, the most important thing to understand is that you have choices. Changing your dominant mindset from Frankenstein to Einstein is one of those *choices* and the following four Innercises employed consecutively in one sitting can facilitate your transition:

1. *Reset your system:* Learn and practice calming your circuits using the Take 6 Innercise.

2. *Increase awareness:* Become aware of your inner Frankenstein using the What's Going on Here? Innercise.

3. *Improve your self-talk:* Learn to feed the positive with the Kill the ANTS Innercise.

4. *Strengthen your agility:* Learn to shift from negative to positive thoughts and emotions, from disempowering to empowering ones, and from destructive to constructive habits and emotions with the Flip-flop Innercise.

1. System Reset

Shifting to a positive mindset begins not with simply "becoming more positive" but with calming your neurology.

This reset can then usher in the next step to increase your awareness of more empowering choices. A great method for starting your reset is the Take 6 Innercise.

"TAKE 6: Calm the Circuits"

Take six deep rhythmic breaths in through your nose and out through your mouth, like you are blowing out of a straw. As you breathe in, say,

I breathe in calmness, I breathe out stress.
or
I breathe in calmness, I breathe out fear.
or
I breathe in calmness, I breathe out anxiety, or overwhelm.

As you continue to take gentle breaths in through your nose and out through your mouth, see and feel what your life will be like when you choose to embrace an empowering, positive mindset.

2. Become Aware of Your Inner Frankenstein

Once you've calmed yourself, validate your awareness: You and all others on the planet have an evolutionary predisposition toward negativity for self-preservation. In addition, it's a neural pattern that you've autonomously reinforced, both consciously and subconsciously, through your life experiences. Becoming *aware* of those patterns you have created and maintained is the starting point for making different choices. That can lead to unraveling your tangle of genetic predispositions and to steering toward more favorable choices. Perhaps you are thinking *my genes are what they are and so I am what I am.* Actually, not so. *Your genes are not the final arbiter in all situations.* There are many circumstances when genetics can be overridden by raising your level of awareness, to the point of first observing your thoughts, emotions, sensations, and behaviors and then, second, modifying them for more favorable outcomes.

. . . .

INNERCISE: What's Going on Here?

Gently, seamlessly transition from the Take 6 Innercise to the What's Going on Here? Innercise and then ask yourself the following questions:

- What's going on here?
- What am I feeling?

- What am I thinking?

- What do I notice about my body? Is my heart rate slow? Fast? Is my breathing shallow? Deep?

- Are the negative and disempowering thoughts, feelings, fears, and anxieties I'm experiencing based in truth, or am I letting my inner Frankenstein take charge with fabrications or old memories?

· ·

3. Improve Your Self-Talk

The next step is to actively and consciously release those negative and disempowering thoughts, feelings, fears, and anxieties.

ANTS is an acronym for "Automatic Negative Thoughts." It's a perfect description of what's going on in the brain of a Debbie Downer or Doubting Dennis. For them, these harmful neural patterns have become default positions—automatic and predictable. For example,

"I did that before and got hurt."

"It might be good for now, but it'll never last."

"I'm not going to risk my reputation over something that might fail."

ANTS can also relate to how a Debbie Downer or Doubting Dennis feel about others:

"They'll never change."

"They're stuck up."

"They'll do just about anything for a buck."

The Kill the ANTS Innercise, based on the work of Dr. Daniel Amen, MD, is specifically helpful for changing these patterns.

. . . .

INNERCISE: Kill the ANTS

1. *Capture the ANTS.* Write down your automatic negative and disempowering thoughts as you have them.

2. *Question them.* Ask yourself, "Are these thoughts *true?*"

3. *Talk back!* If the thoughts *aren't* true, then say so. On the same page that you have written down your ANTS, next to them write down *evidence showing that they're not true.*

4. *Go positive! Repeat empowering affirmations* that are the opposites of your ANTS. In essence, flip your "inner" switch from negative to positive.

This Innercise helps replace ANTS with APTS—*Automatic Positive Thoughts!*—or in other words your Inner Einstein:

- This can work!
- People value my opinion.
- I'm the kind of person who doesn't give up.
- I can figure this out.
- I can learn this.
- I'm willing to try again.

. . . .

4. Practice Switching

Your goal isn't to *eliminate* your Inner Frankenstein—after all, a healthy dose of skepticism, learning from past mistakes, and an understanding of what's realistic are essential tools for a fulfilling life—but rather (a) to become aware of when it's dominating your mindset, and b) to be able to switch in and out of that mindset *so that it best serves you.*

So now that you have a foundation in place for APTS—*Automatic Positive Thoughts!*—the Flip-flop Innercise can help increase your ability to switch between your Inner Frankenstein and Einstein like you would TV shows with a click of the remote control.

. . . .

INNERCISE: The Flip-Flop

First, just a brief refresher: When you activate your Inner Einstein, you reduce activity in your Inner Frankenstein, and vice versa. This is how your brain maximizes its use of its limited resources. This Innercise is designed to help take you to a whole other level, like from chess to three-dimensional chess.

So, begin with choosing a goal. For example, let's use a financial goal for the step-by-step description below.

1. Set a financial goal for increasing your income. Pick a new target annual income that represents a significant, but not impossible, increase. Perhaps to increase your income by 25 percent, or by a specific dollar amount.

2. Write down all of the reasons why you think and feel you **cannot** achieve this goal. For example,

   • *My company will never give me a raise.*

   • *The economy isn't strong enough.*

   • *I don't have the education to find a better job.*

- *I'm really not the competitive type.*
- *I'm not smart enough.*
- *I don't have the money*
- *I don't have the time.*

3. Next, on a different page, write down all of the ways you can think of that could help you achieve this goal. For example,

   - *I'll meet with my manager about taking on more responsibility.*
   - *I'll map out my own plan inspired by others I want to emulate.*
   - *I'll take a part-time course.*
   - *I'll become more resourceful.*
   - *I'll learn whatever I must learn.*
   - *I'll make time.*
   - *I'll find the money.*

Include filling in the blanks for these two statements:

- *I'll ask_____ for help.*
- *I'll research _____.*

These steps can help you get comfortable moving from unhealthy pessimism to healthy optimism. When you feel yourself getting caught in a disempowering thought or emotional pattern, engage with this four-tier process:

1. System reset

2. What's going on here?

3. Kill the ANTS

4. The Flip-Flop

With practice you can become highly skilled at recognizing disempowering patterns and creating new and empowering mindsets: ones that you can reasonably expect to lead you to a fulfilling life. The positivity that can result will further cause the release of the neurochemicals dopamine, serotonin, and others associated with feeling happier, and healthier, thinking clearer and learning faster. Happiness itself can extend your life span, improve your relationships, and generate more financial security.

. . . .

Here is one more very powerful process we teach our clients. It's called **The 4R Innercise.** Whenever you feel any self-doubt, fear, anxiety, stress, or are faced with a disempowering situation, do this:

"TAKE 6: Calm the Circuits"

Take six deep rhythmic breaths in through your nose and out through your mouth, like you are blowing out of a straw. As you breathe in, say,

I breathe in calmness, I breathe out stress.
or
I breathe in calmness, I breathe out fear.
or
I breathe in calmness, I breathe out anxiety, or overwhelm.

Now begin the 4R Innercises process:

1. **Recognize:** Be aware of **your** negative or disempowering thoughts, emotions or past experiences that you may be ruminating on.

   Be mindful, be reflective and be in the moment and surrender. Allow whatever you are experiencing to just be, as you observe it without judgment.

2. **Reframe:** Reframe the unpleasant or unwanted thought or emotion into a positive one by adding words to the emotion or thought or by getting curious and reframing the meaning of it. For example, if you catch yourself talking negatively, just be aware and say to yourself, *WOW, that's so interesting how my brain came up with a negative thought. I now choose to release it and be positive.*

   "Play" with the idea or emotion with you controlling it versus it controlling you. If you are angry or feel victimized by something, instead of dwelling on it, say this to yourself:

   - "Because of this feeling or situation, I am choosing to rise above it and will use it to grow and learn."

   - "Because he did this, or she said that, I choose to be in control and not allow it to affect me."

   - "As a result of this happening to me, I choose to find the positive lesson in this opportunity."

Anytime you reframe something negative or unpleasant into something that empowers you, you are in control versus being a victim.

3. **Release:** Emotions usually only last 90 seconds when you observe them without judgment and gently breathe in and out. (Take 6 Innercise.) Many people create and reinforce disempowering emotional loops by getting sucked into thinking about what they are feeling. Then...they feel what they are thinking about and unknowingly create a self-fulfilling disempowering doom loop that gets reinforced and cemented deeper and deeper into their subconscious.

Practice observing your thoughts and emotions and release them using your take 6 breathing Innercise. Take deep rhythmic breaths in through your nose and out through your mouth and become an observer of your thoughts and emotions.

4. **Retrain:** Create and reinforce a new neural-pattern by:

   • Use positive, polar opposite affirmations and visualize and emotionalize the new thought and feeling you want to have

   • Create an emotional anchor by celebrating each time you catch yourself interrupting any pattern you do not want and replacing it with one you do.

   • Anchor the new thought or emotional pattern with a fist pump and say a power word like YA! or YES! out loud to add emotion and make yourself feel more empowered.

Find as many ways as you can to celebrate your aware-ness and then reinforce your new thoughts, emotions and reframes with a power word and gesture of your own.

Remember...awareness gives you choice and choice is what gives you freedom. Choose powerful thoughts, emotions, and meanings and then choose your behaviors.

Real People. Real Results.

After years of having a safe and secure job as a bank manager, Chris was fired. With a wife, two kids, and a mortgage payment to make, all the fears and worries of the world rested on his shoulders.

As a way to earn income, he spent the next six months as an UBER driver chauffeuring NBA players, celebrities, and successful business people. While he enjoyed what he was doing, it wasn't enough to provide security for his family. It wasn't what he wanted to do for the rest of his life. Chris stumbled across MyNeuroGym.com and joined our free Brain-a-Thon training event. This happened at the same time that he was looking into an opportunity to sell solar solutions door-to-door that caused a lot of fear of rejection for him.

Chris jumped in with both feet and started to Innercise every day and took action based on what he learned in our training videos and the daily coaching we provide in our community. He says, "I have seen a major change in the way I face adversity. I have secured confidence as I engage in work and in my social life. I have seen a major improvement in my relationship with my wife because we have aligned ourselves with the same goals and she has truly become my partner. We enjoy financial peace of mind, which comes from knowing how to access abundance and success in our lives. I now earn $20,000/month, and I plan to triple it." We are so proud of him for bringing financial abundance and security to his life and the life of his family. Chris says, "Recently, my company gave me the opportunity to run an office on my own, and now I can help others acquire the mindset and skills I have learned with NeuroGym."

Chapter Summary and Resources

Summary

- All people have an evolutionary predisposition toward a negativity bias as a way to protect against unknown dangers.

- Your tendency toward disempowering thoughts and feelings is nicknamed your Inner Frankenstein, while your tendency toward empowering thoughts and feelings is nicknamed your Inner Einstein. Both have value. The one you listen to the most is the one that will most shape your life.

- The key to changing your mindset, and the results you strive for, is to strike the right balance between your Inner Frankenstein and Einstein.

- A positive mindset and a healthy construct of emotions are choices available to you.

Additional Free Resources

If you want additional help and free resources on how to best use each section in the book, I'm including some special coaching videos and 9 mini brain-training audios to go along with the book. I will act as your mindset coach as part of buying Innercise. For now, get started with this book and the free resources. Just scan the code below on your smartphone and log in to the NeuroGym platform or go to www.myneurogym.com/innercise to create a log in so you gain access to the free bonuses and resources.

PART III:

Master Your Behavior

"You don't have to be great to start, but you have to start to be great."

—Zig Ziglar

Your Brain on Goals

Nurture Success and Avoid Pitfalls with Brain-Friendly Goals

"Whatever we achieve inwardly will change outer reality."

—Otto Rank

Caroline Sanderson felt as if she'd hit rock bottom. She was a talented hairstylist running her own salon in Inverness, Scotland, but her life was coming apart at the seams.

"It was an incredibly difficult time," she said. "I was a single mom, going through a difficult divorce. I was suffering from terrible back pain. I didn't know how I could make payroll. I really was in a dark place."

Distraught, discouraged, and nearly bankrupt, she looked at her life and the prospect of giving up: "I'm looking around at what I have. I've worked so hard for so many years. I have three children, and I'm on the verge of throwing in the towel on my business." Then she asked herself a question: "Have I really given everything I can?"

The answer was *no*.

That was the turning point for Caroline. "I'd been so distracted by the pain and the struggles. I wanted to know what I was capable of, and make sure I'd given it my all. If I failed and I gave it my all, at least I could say I gave it my best."

But where to begin? For Caroline, beginning meant *deciding what success looked like*. Failure was pretty clear—it meant going out of business. It meant the pain of failure, and the near-constant anxiety of being broke and how this all would affect her kids.

But what was the opposite? What did she *really want*?

To answer that question, she needed a better vision for the future. Caroline discovered our free "Brainathon" training event and her life has never been the same.

The Problem with Goals

Our brains *love* goals. We're hardwired that way. In fact, one of the earliest functions of the primitive nervous system was to sense and trigger movement toward food. Those primitive goal-seeking mechanisms were key to survival then. And today, your *homo sapiens* brain has further evolved to be an advanced goal-setting and prediction machine. You can imagine goals in the distant future that have nothing to do with basic survival. You can think large and get inspired. You can *dream*. There's nothing that distinguishes your inner genius more than the ability to consciously set a goal in the future.

In this chapter, we'll look at exactly what happens to your brain when you set a goal, and how you can Innercise to improve on your natural talent.

Your Innercise Edge: Create Brain-Friendly Goals

The foundation for achieving goals is to *set* them properly in the first place, and that means going a step beyond typical advice. It means setting goals that leverage the power of your brain. And that's exactly what Caroline did when she decided to rededicate herself to growing her business.

One of the first things she did after deciding to give her salon business her all was to start what she called a dream book. Like a diary, her dream book was a private journal she wrote in that captured her goals, dreams, and aspirations. For example, one of her first entries was:

I will become Scottish Hairdresser of the Year.

In Caroline's industry, winning that award would be akin to winning an Oscar. It recognized a stylist who had reached the top of his or her game. For a salon owner on the brink of bankruptcy, whose back pain made it difficult to even work a full day, and with three children she worried about, it was an audacious goal. But she set it anyway.

Setting a "stretch" goal isn't a novel idea, but Caroline took things a step further by developing a more vivid, clear picture of what she wanted. She began to add details to her goal, including clipping out pictures from magazines and then pasting them along with accompanying captions in her dream book. For instance, when she saw a picture in a magazine of a previous year's award winner, she cut it out. To make it even more vivid, she replaced the winner's head with a picture of her own! Images, tiny details, vivid descriptions, photographs, and clippings—they all went into her dream journal.

In addition, she also began to visualize herself winning other awards, and attempting each day to *feel* what her dream would be like to win the big one. She imagined herself at an award ceremony down to every detail: her hairstyle, her outfit, her smile talking with others at the award winner's table, and more. To add strength to her visualizations, she pictured a very famous hairdresser "and I would tell myself that I would be at the same level as them. I would picture myself walking through this very busy room from the back."

It's easy to be fooled into dismissing what Caroline was doing as just wishful thinking. But there's more to this than that. At a neurological level, Caroline was training her brain through an Innercise process we call "cognitive priming."

By reviewing and focusing regularly on her goals in vivid detail, she was helping her conscious mind take more control in aligning with her subconscious mind. Here's how this works.

1. **It Starts with an Idea:** *Left Prefrontal Cortex and Visual Cortex*

   Like Caroline's goal to become Scottish Hairdresser of the Year, every goal you have begins as an idea. From the simple idea such as dropping off shirts at the dry cleaners on Thursday to putting a man on the moon within the decade, everything starts as a thought.

   Setting a goal activates your left prefrontal cortex (PFC). It's a relatively new part of your brain, evolutionarily speaking, that sits right behind your forehead. Your left PFC, among other things, is your idea center—it's the seat of your creative "inner Einstein." When you're generating ideas, coming up with solutions, it's your left prefrontal cortex—your inner Einstein, or CEO is at work.

The left PFC, however, also needs some help from other parts of your brain. In particular, your whole brain is heavily dependent on visual information. To hunt, forage, mate, and survive, vision was absolutely critical in prehistoric times, and even with evolution, today, your brain is still picture-crazy. It needs a clear mental image of what it is you're trying to accomplish. Without it, your brain is limited in how to best take action.

This means abstract ideas or unclear goals have to be turned into concrete images that are shaped by your *visual cortex* located in the back of your brain. If you lean back in your chair, put your feet up on a desk, and lace your fingers behind your head, your hands would be roughly over your visual cortex. This is your "mind's eye," where you see and visualize a goal as if you have actually achieved it.

With both your left PFC and your visual cortex, your brain now has the first and most essential piece of the goal puzzle: *a very specific target to aim for.*

2. **Ready for Action: *Motor Cortex and Blood Pressure***

From your brain's perspective, goals and actions tend to go hand in hand. If you want a glass of water, you'll need to reach for it. If you want to walk, run, lay down, or shake hands, the thought needs to be accompanied by action. For that reason, your goal doesn't just turn on your left PFC, it also stimulates your *premotor regions*—areas of the brain associated with physical movement. And to prepare for those possible movements, it elevates your systolic blood pressure resulting in blood pumping throughout your body and the brain gearing you up to take action.

3. Your Identity: *The Parietal Lobe*

Your brain has another trick up its neurological sleeve. One that you probably aren't aware of. Information about the "mind's eye" image of the goal you set also travels to the *parietal lobe*, one of several areas in the brain that help to create your sense of self—to, in effect, help define who you think you *are*.

It's at this moment that a key shift happens. Because your brain can't tell the difference between the real and the imagined, the goal conjured up in your visual cortex and left PFC has, as far as some parts of your brain are concerned, *already been achieved and already been accepted into your self-image.*

4. Motivation: *Dopamine and the Nucleus Accumbens*

When we set goals that promise rewards such as food, money, sex, or anything else we associate with pleasure—the nucleus accumbens releases a neurotransmitter called *dopamine.* To be clear, the promise of reward releases dopamine, just as the actual experience of the reward does. Dopamine is the fuel in your motivational tank. When you set your goal, the released dopamine travels to your frontal lobe where it gives you the motivation and ability to plan and develop strategies and then to take action.

In addition to stepping on the pedal, at this point your brain also gives you extra acceleration by taking its foot off your neurological brakes. The "brakes" in this case are the worry centers located in the *right prefrontal cortex* and the fear centers in the *amygdala*. When these areas of the brain are active—when you're afraid, anxious, or doubtful—they can cut off the supply of dopamine, as well as other feel-good neurotransmitters such as *oxytocin and serotonin*— draining the fuel from your motivational tank, and instead use the stress hormone cortisol to push you into fight, flight, freeze, or faint. Anytime you've been excited about a goal and then someone deflates your idea by pointing out all the reasons why it won't work, you've likely felt this dampening effect. The same thing can happen when you have an inspiring idea, and you self-sabotage: "Oh. I can't afford that." The brakes go on and you slow to a crawl or maybe even screech to a halt.

But as you now know from our discussion about the Inner Frankenstein, these brakes are also your friend. If you had no worry or fear, you'd make some decisions that wouldn't serve you well. So our best intention is to find a balance between the brakes and the accelerator—between the Inner Frankenstein and the Inner Einstein.

Pitfalls: Goals Gone Wild

There are three common pitfalls in the goal-setting stage. Make any of them, and your goal has a higher likelihood of either failing to align and engage your brain, or, worse, inhibiting your creativity and motivation altogether.

Mistake #1: Lack of Clarity

Your brain needs a clear target, and that means your goal needs to be *precise*, *vivid*, and *in writing*.

You need to be precise.

Remember that you're giving your brain the instructions of what you want it to focus on. "Get my life together" isn't a goal that's specific enough to crank up your Einstein brain.

So instead, consider what specific area of your life you want to improve. Your health? Your finances? Your relationships?

Now, ask yourself: *What specifically do I want to achieve?* Caroline wanted to win the Scottish Hairdresser of the Year award. Declare how much weight you want to lose *and* keep off, and by when? State your debt-free date. Specify the amount of income you want.

When it comes to your achieving your goals, zeroing in on the bull's eye is half the journey.

You need to be vivid.

Remember that your brain can't tell the difference between something you vividly imagine and something that is real. The more vividly you can imagine your goal in all its colors, sounds, smells, senses, emotional contexts, and more, the more clearly your brain can help you make it a reality.

The entries in Caroline's dream journal helped her develop a clearer vision of her future, one that she continued to refine with meditation, and with other Innercises we'll explore in the next chapter.

You need to commit in writing.

Dominican University of California psychology professor Dr. Gail Matthews set out to examine the role of written goals, commitment, and accountability. In her research, individuals with written clear goals achieved their goals 50 percent more often than those without written goals.[29]

Caroline's first entry in her dream book was a written one: *I will become Scottish Hairdresser of the Year.* From there she continued to add to her journal regularly.

You too can turn unclear or abstract goals into concrete images for your brain to take action on by writing out your thoughts. It may take many drafts, but with each one, you can crystallize your image. Simply saying, "It's all up here" and pointing to your head is a bit like chasing your tail. So, choose not to run around in circles by taking the thoughts about your goals out of your head and putting them in clear writing.

Mistake #2: Lack of Emotional Value

Clarity is a critical start to creating a powerful goal, but it doesn't explain why we can be crystal clear about a goal and still fail to do anything about it. All of us at times have known *exactly* what we need to do in order to accomplish a goal, but still failed to *do* it? To understand this in whole, start with the piece on how your brain places value on what's important.

In every moment of your waking day, your brain is juggling options and making decisions. Should I keep working or stop for lunch? Should I go to sleep or stay up for Stephen Colbert? Should I go to the gym or out for drinks?

You are faced with an average of 35,000 remotely conscious decisions every day and your brain needs to process which options are best and how to act on them. In addition, your subconscious weighs in too. Overall, the process involves placing a "value" on things to help make these decisions.

That valuation process is a complicated one. Your brain might use memory information from the hippocampus: "Hey. We did this before, and something good/bad happened." It might use fear information from the amygdala: "That's a threat! This is safer!" It might use the novelty-detection of the hippocampus: "*Hmm.* That's new." And it might use conscious goal information from your left prefrontal cortex.

In the case of a new goal, it becomes critical to ensure that your goal is inspiring enough to "win" the release of dopamine to fuel constructive action. You can do that by ensuring you tie your goal to a meaningful purpose.

You might have a crystal clear vision of your life when you triple your income—from the new house right down to the vacation in Bali. But if that vision isn't something you're emotionally inspired by, you likely won't take the action needed to make this higher income a reality. This means that *you need to combine the mental images you craft about yourself with powerful emotions backing those images.* This winning combination can create a response that is stronger than what is really happening in your life and give you the fortitude to persist when the going gets tough.

A goal that has the deepest meaning, purpose, and value to you is one that you will be most motivated to achieve. It's the one that your nucleus accumbens will decide is your *why*.

For Caroline, it was an easy decision. Her children. "No one else was going to look after me or my children. They were my why. I wanted to know what I was capable of, and make sure I'd given it my all for my children."

Like Caroline, your *why* is your emotional fuel, and you need to top up the tank. Does it matter to you if your life has real purpose or meaning? Will it matter to you if you live your life and reach the end of it feeling like you could have done more? More for yourself? For your family and loved ones? The planet?

. . . .

INNERCISE: Neural Linking and Anchoring

The goal of this Innercise is to link and anchor as many mental images, emotions, feelings, and sensations to your goal. Say, for example, that you want to earn an extra $25,000 in the next six months. Type or write out this number and paste it on a dream or vision board. Next to it, add the words "I am so grateful and happy that I have now earned an extra $25,000."

Now, add to your dream or vision board pictures of friends, family, charities, or anyone else or any other causes that motivate you to achieve this goal. Add your favorite colors or inspiring symbols. Also choose powerful anchor words like "DO IT" and paste them on.

Add anything that motivates you. If there is music you love, listen to it as you review, read, and visualize yourself achieving your goals. If you like a certain scent, write it on your dream board, and then get a little bottle of it and smell it as you read and emotionalize your vision and goals. Personally,

I love smelling lemon and peppermint oils. I use my diffuser to anchor these scents as I read and emotionalize my goals.

Once you have some or all of these items in place, "prime your brain" once or twice a day with these images, emotions, scents, power words, music, and other inspirations. The more senses you engage and the more consistent you are in doing this, the faster and more powerful your neural links will become. You can also use tapping to anchor your goal with this favorable neural linking—use your non- dominant hand and gently tap on your temples or forehead.

. . . .

Mistake #3: The Wrong Size of Goal

Your ancient brain houses an important piece of neuro-logical real estate called the *hypothalamus*. It controls your body's basic essentials like hunger, thirst, and temperature, as well as your stress responses and reproductive hormones.

One of its most important jobs is supporting *homeostasis*— the tendency for your body to stay comfortable and in balance. For example, your internal body temperature stays at around 98.6 degrees, no matter the outside temperature.

The pursuit of homeostasis means that the hypothalamus works a bit like a thermostat in the body, monitoring when things change and then sending signals to restore normalcy. This is truly a remarkable system. But there is a downside. The hypothalamus also makes big changes unwelcome. So, when you set a goal that involves a large change, your hypothalamus counters by trying to bring you back to homeostasis.

We can see this at work when we measure blood pressure in people as they set goals. You may recall from an earlier chapter that your systolic blood pressure rises when you set well-thought out goals. This increase gives you a way of measuring "goal readiness." Unreasonable goals that are too hard *or* too easy create a lower systolic blood pressure boost—meaning you're less goal-ready[30]—than goals that are just right.

Goals, then, have a neurological sweet spot. Too big a perceived change, and your hypothalamus and amygdala get involved, ramping up your stress response and leading you to fight, flight, freeze, or faint. Too *small* a goal and you simply aren't motivated enough to take action toward achieving it. In both cases, your nucleus accumbens tends to decide that your dopamine would be better used for maintaining the status quo.

Right in the middle, between "too much" and "too little" change is the sweet spot. To find your sweet spot, you'll have to experiment with goals that are challenging enough to inspire a dopamine release that helps spur you to take action, but ones you still perceive as *possible,* so you don't rouse your hypothalamus or amygdala.

In addition to the positive focus on your sweet spot, you also need to visualize and emotionalize overcoming real inner and outer obstacles that might keep you from reaching your goals. There is an Innercise designed for this and it is called mental contrasting. *Mental contrasting* can energize your frontal lobe in a way that motivates your brain to take action as well as turn your desire into an *expectation.*[31]

A Dream (Book) Come True

When you go through day after day without clear intentions, when you let your mind wander and old habits reign supreme, when you allow fear and anxiety to rule over rational decision-making, you essentially concede the high ground to the autopilot. This is one critical reason why goals are important.

Goals tell your brain what to do. Without them, you give away control and the opportunity for change becomes a roll of the dice. By setting goals the *right* way, you can engage in a lifelong process of growth, just as Caroline discovered.

By 2018 a lot had changed in Caroline's life—almost everything, it seemed. Once nearly bankrupt, she'd dramatically transformed her business and finances, at one point realizing that she'd reached over a million US dollars in assets. She was "officially," she likes to say playfully, a millionaire.

Along the way she'd won a series of major industry awards, overcome a fear of public speaking, and built a spin-off enterprise helping other salon owners transform their own businesses. At one memorable award ceremony, she even found herself walking from the back of a busy room to accept an award alongside a famous industry hairdresser— the same room and hairdresser as she had envisioned in her dream book. In November 2017 Caroline and a colleague attended a posh industry event at the Grosvenor House Hotel in London. There, in front of 2,000 stylists, they took the stage and accepted the award for Scottish Hairdresser of the Year.

She credits her three months of brain training with helping her build the habits she needed to reach her goal. Her ability to create vivid, inspiring intentions for her life had paid off. "It really was about changing on the inside. You learn to deal with things differently. It's not a magic wand, but you know that you're strong enough to handle things. It wasn't overnight, but gradual, one opportunity after another."

Goals as Means, Not Ends

Caroline, however, is the first to admit that goals alone are not enough: "The visualization was important. But it's always paired with action. That has to be part of it. I had to study. I would work for hours after the kids were in bed. It wasn't just writing in a dream book."

Caroline's emphasis on action mirrors something I often tell people after they've set a goal: *Hope is not a strategy.* While a crystal clear, inspiring goal is powerful, it's not the *whole* picture.

Research supports this. If we spend all our time fantasizing about our future success, it can actually inhibit our action in the present. In one study, for example, job seekers who spent the most time fantasizing applied for fewer jobs, got fewer offers, and were offered lower salaries.[32]

So, to translate your goals into action, you'll need a brain-friendly action plan to get you from where you are to where you want to be—and that's exactly where we're headed next.

. . . .

INNERCISE: Goal-Setting

Find a comfortable space where you won't be disturbed for about forty-five minutes.

Step 1: Get in the right mindset.

Get comfortable and let go of "how" for now. Give yourself permission to dream freely and look into the future.

Imagine you're ninety years old. You're reaching the end of your life, and now, on a beautiful day, you're sitting in a rocking chair on the front porch of your home. Many years have passed, and you're reflecting back on your life.

What would your older, wiser self say to who you are now? What would your older, wiser self, tell you to stop doing? To start doing? What would your older, wiser self, tell you to start now so that when you do reach ninety, you'll have lived the most amazing life?

Step 2: Take ten to fifteen minutes and write down one goal or vision for your life.

- Be specific and vivid in your description.

- Don't think about *how* you will achieve this. Instead, allow yourself to create a mindset of infinite possibilities.

Step 3: Take five minutes and emotionalize this one goal or vision for your life. Write down your answers to the following questions:

- Why *must* I achieve my goal?

- What will I gain?
- What are the consequences of *not* achieving my goal?
- How will I feel when I achieve it?
- How will I feel if I *don't?*
- Who will benefit when I achieve it, and who may suffer if I do not?

Next, play a mental movie with your eyes open or closed in which you see yourself victorious in having achieved your goal.

. . . .

Real People. Real Results.

At 66 years young, Joanie Sanderson worked for many years helping families in her outback hometown in New South Wales, Australia. Although she loved her work, she never felt comfortable accepting money for her services. Joanie was widowed and she raised their eight kids herself—a feat made more impressive because she did it all on her widower's pension of $12,000 a year.

For many years, Joanie's only income goals were simply survival goals—to put a roof over her family's head, gas in the car, and food on the table. Any aspirations she had beyond that seemed to fade away in the face of the realities of trying to live below the poverty line.

As her kids grew, left home, and had kids of their own, Joanie began to see a new ambition on the horizon. Now a grandmother, Joanie's dream was to take her grandchildren to Disneyland with her daughter.

It wasn't long before the realities of the plan set in: a trip for all of them to Disney would easily cost more than an entire year of her income.

Joanie still worked as a counselor, but due to her low self-worth, she gave away almost 90 percent of her services for free, as she always had. She knew her work was valuable and she made a big difference for her clients, but she didn't feel right asking for money. Even if she saved every single penny and lived for free, Joanie wasn't likely to get to Disneyland anytime soon.

Not long after, Joanie found MyNeuroGym.com. With nothing to lose, she began to Innercise daily using the brain training audios NeuroGym has for winning the game of money.

Within a year, everything began to change. In her sixties, the woman who'd never earned more than a widower's pension of $12,000 was now earning more than $75,000 a year. New doors have opened, her poverty mindset is totally gone, and her dream vacation with her family became a reality.

Chapter Summary and Resources

Summary

- Goals can help align your conscious and subconscious minds.

- Goals can give your brain a target to aim for.

- Vivid, precise, and written goals are more achievable than those that are not.

- There's a neurological sweet spot for right-sized goals whereas ones that are too large or too small likely will not be rewarded.

- Creating an achievable daily action plan for your goals increases the likelihood of success.

Additional Free Resources

If you want additional help and free resources on how to best use each section in the book, I'm including some special coaching videos and 9 mini brain-training audios to go along with the book. I will act as your mindset coach as part of buying Innercise. For now, get started with this book and the free resources. Just scan the code below on your smartphone and log in to the NeuroGym platform or go to www.myneurogym.com/innercise to create a log in so you gain access to the free bonuses and resources.

Make the Plan

Feeding Your Brain with Success

"The man who moves a mountain begins by carrying away small stones."

—Attributed to Confucius, Chinese philosopher

Imagine you're tasked with the job of getting a group of people to exercise at least once a week. You know from experience that even one exercise session a week is difficult to get people to maintain. So how would you do it? Without paying them, punishing them, or forcing them, how would you get a group of couch potatoes to change their ways?

Using some good old psychology, you could probably come up with a few ideas. For example, you might

1. *Measure:* by asking people to track their exercise each day.

2. *Motivate:* by handing out some information on how exercise combats heart disease.

3. *Plan:* by asking people to write down in advance specifically when and where they would actually exercise.

These are all tried and true approaches for getting people to take action toward a goal. But which works the best? For researchers who did a similar experiment,[33] their results are pretty astonishing:

- Group 1 (measure) exercised at least once a week 38 percent of the time.

- Group 2 (measurement plus motivation) exercised at least once a week 35 percent of the time.

- Group 3 (measurement, motivation, and planning) exercised at least once a week an amazing 98 percent of the time!

That's right. Planning was the "X" factor. In fact, as you can see, using motivation without planning (Group 2) actually *reduced* the number of people who exercised. To be clear, these weren't complicated plans. All that the researchers asked Group 3 to do was fill in the blank on one simple statement:

During the next week, I will partake in at least twenty minutes of exercise on [DAY] at [TIME OF DAY] at/in [PLACE].

That's it. A simple sentence completion involving planning, and participants were able to nearly triple their success rate beyond motivational approaches alone. Seem too good to be true? Not once you understand how planning affects your brain, and how Innercise can help you leverage it.

This is Your Brain on Plans

If you've ever attended a seminar and been inspired to make great change, only to find yourself right back where you started, you've again experienced the enormous gap that exists between setting goals and actually reaching them. Whether you're trying to do something as simple as exercise once a week, like the people in the previous study, or whether you're trying something as daunting as leaving your career job to start a business, that gap is always there.

Plans can help bridge that gap between goals and achievement. And *without plans, your goals are really just dreams.* The reason plans work so well is because of the way they impact the brain. Here are four distinct reasons why Innercising your "mental planning muscle" can make all the difference.

1. HOW and WHY work differently in the brain

In the last chapter, we looked at the idea that goals with a high emotional value can "win" dopamine from the nucleus accumbens. That dopamine is the "brain fuel" that helps motivate you.

If you set a goal with a powerful *why*, you experience that first dopamine hit. But while that *why* is critically important to creating your goals, it's only a first step on the road to accomplishing them.

When researchers at the University of California in Los Angeles looked at the brains of people to understand the difference between "how" and "why," they found that as far as the brain is concerned, they are two very different things.[34] Thinking about *why* we're doing something activates a very separate region of the brain from how region. When you think about how to accomplish a task, such as cooking a meal, you engage areas on the left side of the brain that involve planning movements and orienting positions—in this example: you, ingredients, and cooking tools—in a physical space. But when you focus on why you do something, you activate different parts of your brain altogether, ones associated with thinking about mental states and intentions.

This all makes sense—why and how are indeed very different things. But here's what's so important about this distinction: *It seems we can't do both at the same time.*

Your brain is incredibly efficient. It has to be in order to get everything done. Part of that efficiency, as we looked at earlier, comes from automating things below the level of consciousness through systems and habits. But another way the brain seems to be efficient is by reducing activity in one area when another is active. In the case of *how* and *why*, the brain isn't good at doing both at once.

This is a theme that crops up again and again in the brain—when you activate one region, you can inhibit another. It's why the Einstein/Frankenstein divide is so important. When your inner Frankenstein takes over, there's a good chance your Inner Einstein is being shut down at the same time, and vice versa.

It seems, then, that the old saying, "Where there's a will, there's a way," isn't quite accurate. Where there's a will, we also need to *create* a clear way. We need to make sure we activate not just the parts of the brain that help us create the goal but also the parts of the brain that help get us there. Spend all your time in "why" and you're a dreamer who never takes action. Spend all your time in "how" and you might be busy, but with what?

When you activate these various parts, an important switch takes place. You move from your conscious mind to your subconscious mind—you move from the realm of imagination, to the realms of beliefs, actions, and, eventually, productive habits.

2. Your brain thrives on the mini-success of plans

The initial boost of dopamine you get from setting a goal is helpful. And, as we'll see, you can continue to support your efforts by focusing on your goal. But that's not enough.

There's a good chance your big goal is *too* big, at least to bite off at once. Big change is almost always a long-term project, and for that, you need the on-going motivation that comes from regular dopamine infusions. The jolt of setting the goal isn't enough, just like flooring the gas pedal only once in your car won't get you very far. You need a steady supply of infusions to power a long journey.

Fortunately, that delivery method is prewired into your brain. Every time you succeed at something, your brain releases more dopamine. It's a reward system designed to keep you doing more of what works, and less of what doesn't.

You can feel this tiny burst every time you sense the satisfaction of ticking something off your to-do list. In fact, if you've ever added something to your to-do list that you've already done just to have the satisfaction of ticking it off, you've truly experienced how compelling a small win can be.

The secret to those tiny bursts is a clear plan created from small steps. Each baby step success provides a dopamine boost that motivates you to take another step, and on and on. With enough doable steps, you can create a virtuous cycle that ensures you have a steady supply of motivational fuel to reach your goal.

3. Goals are loose ends in the brain

One of the surprising paradoxes of change is that goals can actually distract you from...well, reaching your goals.

Because your brain is so goal-oriented, it keeps focusing on your goals even when you're not actively working toward them. When you want something and you don't yet have it, your brain continues to allocate resources to "keeping the goal alive" until you can accomplish it.

This would be fine if we only had one goal to think about. In reality, your daily life is filled with a multitude of goals of wildly varying sizes. Even the act of brushing your teeth is fulfilling a goal.

The result is that goals become a kind of loose end in the brain, and those loose ends can distract us from the work of actually tying them up. It's a surprising contradiction, but one we have to resolve in the brain. While Einstein is consciously trying to direct you to focus on your big idea, Frankenstein may have catalogued dozens of other ideas that are each using up valuable bandwidth.

The best solution for this is planning.

4. Your two brains are time-conflicted

Imagine that you've set a goal to lose weight. To accomplish this, you've decided to change your diet. Setting the goal has likely inspired you, yet, almost without realizing it, you find yourself adding less-healthy choices to your shopping cart or sitting in front of the TV with a bowl of something sugary. What happened? How can you be so motivated in one moment and so off-track the next?

The culprit in this case is how different areas of your brain view *time*. You see, parts of your brain have the ability to set goals for the future while other parts are more inclined toward immediate gratification. Once again, planning is the bridge. A good plan tells you what to do next. Without one, you can feel a void that you're likely to fill by reaching for default unhealthy habits you've been stockpiling over the years.

. . . .

INNERCISE: True North

Have paper and a writing instrument on hand.

Start with the Innercise Take 6. Get into a totally relaxed, calm, peaceful state of mind and being. Be aware of your thoughts, emotions, feeling, and sensations without any judgment.

. . . .

. . . .

INNERCISE. "TAKE 6: Calm the Circuits"

Do this now:

Take six deep rhythmic breaths in through your nose and out through your mouth, like you are blowing out of a straw. As you breathe in, say,

> *I breathe in calmness, I breathe out stress.*
> *or*
> *I breathe in calmness, I breathe out fear.*
> *or*
> *I breathe in calmness, I breathe out anxiety, or overwhelm.*

Now, think of one goal that you really want to achieve. It can be a health goal, a financial goal, a relationship goal, career or business goal, or even a goal to travel somewhere in the world.

Allow your thoughts and emotions to flow freely through your mind as you write down your answers to the following questions:

"Am I really committed to achieving this goal? Yes or no?"

If no, choose a different goal until you find one you can answer yes to "Am I really committed to achieving this goal?" From this yes, then springboard to writing down your answers these follow-up questions:

- What needs to happen in order for me to move towards achieving this goal?

- What do I need to learn?

- What skill do I need to upgrade?

- Whose help do I need?

- What must I let go of?

- What must I start?

- What must I stop?

- What do I need to believe about myself in order to achieve this goal?

- What resources do I need to make achieving this goal a reality?

As you answer these questions in a nonjudgmental, unemotional way, you will start seeing a clearer path to the thoughts, feelings, emotions, and behaviors you need to follow to move toward making the goal you want to achieve more real in your mind and in your life. Now, from these answers, choose one thing you can do in the next 24 hours to move toward achieving this goal.

As you continue to breathe in and out gently, set aside some time in the next 24 hours and start developing a road map with easy-to-follow action plans for achieving your goal. Then, put the action steps in your calendar so that each and every day you take a small action step toward it. Make sure to track your progress.

Keep it simple, keep it real, and get into action.

. . . .

Your Way to a Brain-Friendly Plan

As you know from the chapter on habits, the regular small successes that a plan can help you achieve are the building blocks of new habits. In essence your plan isn't just a plan to reach your goal, *it's a training schedule for your brain.* It's an Innercise to train your brain for goal achievement.

In order to bridge the distance between setting your goal and actually accomplishing it, we use an Innercise called "The STT Process." STT is an acronym for *Strategies, Tactics, and Timelines.*

A strategy is something you can do to achieve your goal. If, for example, your goal is to lose weight, there are a number of strategies you can use. You might reduce how much you eat, for example, or you might exercise more.

When you identify a strategy, *you're giving your brain an instructional overview.* A tactic, on the other hand, is far more specific. It's a single, actionable item. If you want to lose weight, for example, and your strategy is to exercise more, there are thousands of tactics you can use. You might

- Go for a walk.
- Ride your bike around the block.
- Hike with your family or friends.

When you create tactics, you break your strategy down into individual action items that (a) are clear and actionable for your brain and (b) make you feel confident you can accomplish them. Tactics are designed to be inherently *doable.*

To make tactics most effective, however, make them time-specific. For example, you might take the tactics above, and add specific dates and times:

- Walk briskly for twenty minutes on Monday at noon.

- Ride my bike for fifteen minutes on Tuesday at 5:30 PM.

- Hike with my family for an hour on Saturday morning at 8 AM.

A good plan has very small, specific tactics. It may not seem lofty, but it's far better to have tiny tactics that you'll actually *do* than large leaps that you'll give up on after just a day or two. The more you Innercise, the bigger the tactics you can succeed at.

. . . .

INNERCISE: The STT Process

In completing the following STT worksheet below:

1. Make sure you're as specific as possible. "Tuesday at 4" is more specific than just "Tuesday."

2. Don't worry if your plan doesn't feel complete. It's normal to not be able to see the entire scope of change at once. Focus on a time period that you feel comfortable with, such as the next week or month.

3. Focus on what you feel is reasonable within that time period. It's far better to have simple tactics that you can actually do, then lofty ones you'll fail at. The habit is more important than the intensity or size!

4. If you stumble in trying to execute your plan, ask yourself, "What's the smallest possible next step?" There's always a tinier next step, and eventually you'll find one that is small enough to begin with.

5. Share your plan with a family member or friend. Or better yet, find an accountability partner. You'll release oxytocin by cooperating with others!

Sometimes You Just Need the Next Step

Life, as they say, is what happens while we're making other plans. Your progress won't always follow your plan—that's normal. In fact, things almost never go *exactly* to plan.

What planning does, however, is let you see at least as far as the next step you need to take. As the author E. L. Doctorow said, "Writing is like driving at night in the fog. You can only see as far as your headlights, but you can make the whole trip that way." Planning gives you headlights. It helps you illuminate the road to where you want to go.

. . . .

Real People. Real Results.

Several years ago, Lisa found herself in a pretty bad situation battling health challenges. Her family was $60,000 in debt and had taken a second mortgage on their home to make ends meet. She was stressed beyond her ability to cope and wasn't sure what would happen next.

Lisa had spent years practicing and certifying as an energy healing expert, who specializes in releasing inherited emotional patterns, but faced one huge stumbling block: she had a fear of people judging her for her profession.

"I was a constant ruminator," she said. "I was stuck in my negative thought patterns and raised with a belief that if I charged people money for my gifts, God would take them away from me."

The result of that fear? Lisa kept her profession as a hobby, never charging for her services.

After watching the Brain-A-Thon, Lisa began Innercising. Slowly, she learned to get over her fear of people's judgement of her profession, and thus her self-esteem, confidence, and life began to change.

Within 4 weeks, she doubled her income from $3,000 to $6,000 per month. And now, at the time of this writing, she's making $25,000 a month doing something she loves! In just one year, Lisa dramatically changed her life by acknowledging her fear, and retraining her brain to use that fear as fuel for her success.

Chapter Summary and Resources

Summary

- Plans are the bridge between setting goals and achieving them. Without them, your goals are just dreams.

- HOW and WHY work differently in the brain. Both require dedicating time to understanding them.

- Small steps allow for mini-successes, which can give you bursts of motivating dopamine.

- Planning is an Innercise. When you do it, you're changing your brain.

- You don't have to know your whole plan at once. Just knowing the next step can be enough to eventually get you to your destination.

Additional Free Resources

If you want additional help and free resources on how to best use each section in the book, I'm including some special coaching videos and 9 mini brain-training audios to go along with the book. I will act as your mindset coach as part of buying Innercise. For now, get started with this book and the free resources. Just scan the code below on your smartphone and log in to the NeuroGym platform or go to www.myneurogym.com/innercise to create a log in so you gain access to the free bonuses and resources.

Your Innercise Ritual

Putting Innercise to Work Every Day

"Don't judge each day by the harvest that you reap but by the seeds that you plant."

—Robert Louis Stevenson

In 2004, author Alan Deutschman was attending a conference at an elite medical research center in New York City. The purpose of the conference was to bring together some of the world's most brilliant minds to collaborate on solving the world's most pressing problems.

The first of those problems was health care, and what Deutschman heard that day, not only unnerved him, but moved him enough to write a book, *Change or Die,* opening with this provocative question:

> *If a trusted authority said you had to make difficult and enduring changes in the way you think, feel, and act or you would DIE…could you do it?*

If you had to exercise every day or die, could you? If you had to change how you felt, what you believed or how you thought consistently, could you? If you had to make the sales calls, let go of a grudge, or be more emotionally available, could you do it if your life depended on it?

Almost everyone will immediately answer: *yes.*

In Deutschman's book, he describes how the experts had pegged the odds of people with debilitating heart disease actually changing their unhealthy behaviors to healthy ones at about one in ten. Even though surgery was only a temporary fix to avoid looming death, 90 percent of these patients literally *couldn't change to save their lives.*

It's a discouraging statistic. But, despite its dramatic name, *Change or Die* is optimistic about people's ability to change. The problem, Deutschman concludes, isn't that people are fundamentally unable to change. It's just that we tend to use the wrong strategies. We aren't broken; we just don't know any better.

Successful Change

Here's how to know better: Innercise to change your brain in order to change your life.

By this point, you might have noticed an interesting conundrum for the brain. We know that the brain affects everything we do. It's a filter of beliefs and mindset and perception—a network of electrical patterns that determine how we think, feel, and act at any moment. But, thanks to the wonders of neuroplasticity, we also know that the opposite is true. The way we think, feel, and act *changes the brain.*

So, the brain changes us, but we also change the brain.

But which comes first? The chicken or the egg? For the answer, we're going to turn to, of all places, Hollywood.

Going Hollywood

When an actor tackles a new part, the job of showing up on the set every day and delivering the lines is just the tip of the iceberg. Before shooting begins, actors can spend months getting ready for a role.

An actor might study their part, reading over their lines each day. They might visualize themselves as the character they're to play. They might research the behaviors, accents, and mannerisms of their character, and may go so far as to change their surroundings to immerse themselves in the role as much as possible. The actor's job during this time period is to, as they sometimes say in the acting world, *become* the role. The more an actor can take on the role of the character they're playing, the more the role comes to life on the screen or stage. But acting is not all glamour as it's often made out to be. The actor's accent might be off. Their acting might be too "on the nose" or the delivery stilted. They might get the mannerisms wrong. And occasionally they might just downright *flop*—flub their lines, or worse, be unable to match the director's vision and end up with most of their scenes on the cutting room floor.

There's a similar process going on when you want to change any part of your lives. I call it *roots and shoots.*

Roots and Shoots

We all want the money, the weight loss, the romantic part-ner, the successful business—and we want them *yesterday.* If there's one thing that almost everyone shares, it's that we want good things to happen *now.* But know this: Everything happens in its own time.

Nature has this figured out—it's called the Law of Gestation. It tells us that just as babies take time to grow, our adult efforts to grow also take time. You can plant a seed this morning, but you're not going to get a harvest this afternoon.

Gestation isn't just about being patient though. It's about understanding that during the time before you see results, *something is still happening.* The seed you planted is begin-ning to change. Even though you can't see *anything* above the surface, there's a lot happening below. Before you see shoots, there are *roots.*

We can see the Law of Gestation at work in the neural pat-terns of the brain. Changing a habit, for example, *takes time.* As we discussed in the earlier chapter on habits, research has shown that it takes between 65 and 365 days to form a new habit that sticks, but that's just an average. It might take you more time or less time; every habit is different, every person unique. The point is new ways of thinking, feeling, and behaving take time.[35]

If you go to the gym once, you don't have a new habit—but you've just planted the first synaptic seeds for a new pattern in the brain. It's going to take more time and effort for the roots to grow, and longer still for the shoots to become visible.

To create a no caffeine habit, or a retirement savings habit, or a journaling habit, you have to plant the seed and continue to nurture it. You need to drink only tea, juice, or water every day. You need to set aside a little every paycheck. You need to write every day. And with each day, the seed takes root and grows a little more.

Roots and Shoots, over time—neural patterns forming and reinforcing over day, week, month   Photo credit: iStockPhoto

Think of the roots as changes in your subconscious brain—they are shifts beneath the level of your awareness. Eventually, these roots will begin to manifest changes that we're consciously aware of. Have faith that the roots are growing beneath the surface. And there is a harvest to come perhaps in the form of you noticing you have more energy. Or you're more positive in your mindset. Or your relationships are going more smoothly.

. . . .

INNERCISE: Flip-Flop—Actor's Studio

This is a variation on the earlier described Flip-Flop Innercise.

Imagine that you are a Hollywood actor. You've just been hired to play a role that requires the skill of shifting from one emotion to another, from one tone of voice to another, and from one behavior to another. You are being paid $10 million and the role is so big, there's already talk you could win an Academy Award for your performance.

To practice for your part, begin by smiling and looking up. Make sure to see and feel the effects of your smiling and looking up with a lot of hope. After you do this for five or six seconds, look down and frown and feel sad without any hope.

After you do this for five or six seconds, shift again to being angry at something or someone. Just bring up the emotion of anger and notice how that makes you feel. Notice your physiology, what your body is doing.

Now switch, like the good Hollywood actor that you are, into feeling happy, focused, and elated. Notice your breathing, your feelings, sensations, and your physiology.

The lesson in doing this powerful Innercise is to discover that you can, at will, choose thoughts, feelings, emotions, and behaviors that will empower you instead of ones that disempower you.

You can do this Innercise to shift from negative disempowering and destructive thoughts, emotions, and behaviors to positive empowering thoughts, emotions, and behaviors. The power is within you; the choice is yours.

The Gap

There is an important lesson about the gap of time between when your roots are first forming, and when your shoots first appear. This will be vulnerable period for you. You're doing the work, but not seeing the results just yet. You might even feel like giving up. Don't! You're doing the *most important work*. You're planting and nurturing mental and emotional seeds, so they can bloom later with the results you desire.

Imagine you start an exercise program. Your goal is to shed 25 pounds, regain your energy, and perhaps even see some of those legendary "abs" that you hear people talk about.

On Day 1, you get up early and go for a long walk. It's the first time you've really exercised in years, and you feel energized. You eat a healthy breakfast, and then head for the bathroom.

First stop, the scale.

Wait a minute, you think. *Something's wrong. My weight hasn't changed at all in the last hour.*

Check the mirror: no abs, either. *What the hell?*

Most of us know intuitively that this is a ridiculous way to approach a change in lifestyle. Of course you're not going to lose 25 pounds and get a six-pack in one morning. You have to eat well and exercise daily, and then gradually the change comes. We all know that.

Yet, expecting instant results is exactly how we often approach change. We want to change our habits, get over our fears, or relieve our anxiety, but we want it *now*. We want the successful business or the new career with a single phone call. We want the increased income or the great relationship with one morning of visualization.

That's not how gestation works. Roots take time and nurturance to become shoots. When you're doing the work but haven't yet seen the results, that's the time to keep going! Plant the seeds, and nurture them daily, and the results will follow.

The key to change is to realize that *staying power* beats *willpower*. Be patient.

· ·

INNERCISE: Hollywood Express

Imagine you are sitting quietly by yourself at a coffee shop, enjoying a latte or tea, reading a newspaper or magazine.

You feel a gentle tap on your shoulder, and as you look up you immediately recognize the face of the person. For a moment you can't believe your eyes: a legendary Hollywood filmmaker is standing there waiting to talk with you!

He says that he has just written a script for a lovely adventure comedy and that you look exactly like the lead character he has imagined would play the part. He goes on to offer you an opportunity to star in this role.

How would this make you feel? Would you be shocked? Elated? Scared and fearful? Would there be some underlying excitement, as you imagined this break of a lifetime?

Regardless of what emotions this causes you to feel, keep taking deep breaths in and out in a calm, rhythmic fashion, and imagine that, after a little more conversation, you accept his offer to star in this amazing role of a lifetime. The possibility to make millions of dollars in this role is real. The possibility to win an Academy Award for this role is real. The possibility to work with the Hollywood elite is real.

Now let me ask you this: Would you be willing to learn how to act if you had amazing acting coaches at your side? Would you be willing to role play over and over and over again until you perfected the lines, the emotions, the cadence, and the character?

I would imagine that to take advantage of this once in a lifetime opportunity you would eat what you needed to eat, you would sleep as many hours as you needed to rest, you would practice as many hours as it took to know the role and become the role. Wouldn't you?

This Hollywood Express Innercise is the exact process you can apply to your own life for the leading role you are already playing. What knowledge or skills must you upgrade to achieve your goals? What feelings and emotions do you have to bring forth and master.

As you continue inhaling and exhaling gently, in through your nose and out through your mouth, be aware of the answers that percolate up to your consciousness. Trust your intuition and the wisdom within, and follow through on those insights with the actions required, each day, each week, and each month.

. . . .

Daily Nurturing: Developing Your Innercise Ritual

The daily planting and nurturing of "neural seeds" is what Innercise is all about. To make sure it happens, have a daily

Innercise Ritual—a prescribed, predictable way to continue to work on your brain. Your brain loves habits. It's a habit-forming machine!

For Innercise to work best, *turn Innercise itself into a daily habit.*

Below are some guidelines for creating your Innercise ritual:

1. Create a Consistent Ritual Time and Place

The best way to forge your Innercise ritual is to engage with it at a consistent time and place every day.

Tips:

- Earlier in your day is better. You don't need to get up at the crack of dawn but, putting your Innercise ritual at the start to your day, not only keeps you focused and positive, but also ensures that it happens *before* anything else might derail you. Most people have more control over the first part of their day, and also feel like they have more attention and willpower.

- Any location will do, provided you're uninterrupted. All you need is a small amount of comfortable space to call your own.

2. Look for Innercise Moments

Watch for moments in your day when you can Innercise. Many of the Innercises take as little time as it takes for three slow, even breaths. You need to breathe anyway, why not make it an Innercise? Any time you want to achieve a goal is an opportunity to Innercise. Innercises are effective for business-building, stress-busting, fear-facing, anxiety-reducing, happiness-sustaining, and more.

3. Record and Review Your Progress

Change is hard. We know that much, but by now you also know it's *possible*. But even as you begin to get closer to achieving your goals with Innercises, there's still a common pitfall that's easy to fall into: failing to *notice* that you're changing. When your shoots first start to appear, it can be easy to overlook them. And as they grow, day-to-day changes can be so subtle they go unnoticed.

Imagine, for example, that you're trying to lose weight. You begin to Innercise, and to start changing your lifestyle. Now imagine that each day you lose just 2 ounces of fat—that's it. Just two *ounces*. It's such a small amount that from day-to-day, you probably wouldn't even notice. In fact, if you weren't paying attention, you might think *nothing* was happening, and that you might as well just give up.

But if you keep going, those little two-ounce bits would add up to more than ten pounds of fat in just three months. More than *forty* pounds in a year! Imagine yourself 40 pounds lighter in a year. Or $40,000 wealthier! Or forty more minutes calmer. These are all changes that are dramatic, but ones that could also happen in ways you might not realize day-to-day.

To make sure you don't miss those changes, it's critically important to find a way to measure and record your progress. When your motivation wanes, or you feel like you're not making progress, you can look back on your results over a longer period of time, and see that, *yes, it really is working.*

4. Stick with Your Workout

Rituals are about consistency. Reviewing and studying your goals and progressing toward them is an essential part of daily Innercise, not a one-time exercise. Because in large part your neuro-muscles get stronger with repetition. Start slowly and give your neuro-muscles time to strengthen through Innercises.

At the heart of your strengthening program is the understanding that taking *action is the best way to build your neuro-muscles.* When you take even the smallest new action, you expose yourself to novelty. You challenge the brain. You learn and grow. Whether you succeed or fail, *you've increased your ability simply by trying.*

Neurofeedback

When your brain cells communicate with each other, they produce electrical impulses called brainwaves. We can use electroencephalography (EEG) to measure those brainwaves and to get a look at what's happening in the brain.

Neurofeedback is a brain training process that lets participants see their brain waves on a screen in real time, and practice using various techniques to help them consciously control their brain activity.

Research shows neurofeedback can be helpful for treating a number of health conditions, including anxiety, ADHD, PTSD, eating disorders, and depression.

. . . .

INNERCISE: The Reframe

Think of an experience you've had in your life that you are not happy with, are ashamed of, or feel guilty about.

Dig deep and ask yourself: *What are three positives about the experience?* For example, what lessons did you learn? What have you done differently since then? Have you used the experience as fuel for success?

. . . .

A Typical Innercise Ritual

Over 100,000 people have used NeuroGym training programs to structure their daily Innercise rituals. Our audio and video–based training programs encompass

- Proprietary Brain Activation Sound Technology
- Guided Imagery & Visualization Techniques
- Metaphorical Stories
- Precision Affirmations/Positive Self-Talk
- Reframing & Anchoring Techniques
- Subliminal Messaging
- Meditation
- Mindfulness training
- Self-Acceptance Training
- Cognitive Dissonance Reduction
- Cognitive Priming Techniques
- Cognitive Behavior Therapy
- New Habit Formation Training
- Neural Rescripting Techniques
- Mental Contrasting Training
- Mindset and Emotional Mastery Training
- Guided Hypnotherapy

You'll want to customize your ritual to make it uniquely yours, but here are some common practices that NeuroGym users incorporate into their days:

- Morning and evening gratitude exercises
- Prayer
- Reading
- Prime your brain by reviewing, visualizing, and emotionalizing your goals
- Meditation
- Exercise
- Innercise to develop and strengthen new beliefs, habits, and emotional anchors
- Review and create plans for the day
- Reflect and think on life
- Identify and consistently do the highest impact activities
- Close the day with gratitude and appreciation

Your ritual will always work better when it has *context*. What I mean is take the time to understand how your daily Innercises fit with your overall plan for your life. An excellent way to see this context is through *My Exceptional Life Blueprint*. It can help you define a vision for your life, identify your goals in key areas, and map out the daily rituals and steps needed to transform your life.

Download your own blueprint and mini-training session at www.myneurogym.com/innercise.

Innercising with Affirmations

Affirmations are short, powerful statements designed to help you interrupt disempowering patterns and replace them with empowering thoughts, feelings, and behaviors. These positive declarations are an extremely helpful part of any Innercise ritual. Here are a few NeuroGym favorites:

- Each day, in every way, I am getting better and better.
- I am inquisitive, creative, fun loving, and adventurous.
- I have the extraordinary ability to accomplish everything I choose and want.
- I am committed, determined and passionate about what I do.
- I am very focused and persistent.
- I have tremendous energy and focus for achieving all my life goals.
- Money flows easily and frequently into my life.
- Today I am more confident than ever before.
- Being healthy is my natural state of being.
- I have an abundance of physical and mental energy, and I look and feel great.
- I am my own authority and I am not affected by negative opinions or attitudes of others.
- It is not what happens to me, but how I handle it, that determines my emotional well-being.
- I love my body, mind, and spirit.
- I can earn the income I choose.
- I am smart and deserving of success.

You Are Not the Scorecard

When the shoots of a plant don't meet our expectations, we don't blame the plant. We look to the seeds, the water, or the sun. We look to how the shoots were nurtured. Were the weeds pulled out? Was the soil tilled?

The same applies to your own shoots. They are simply scorecards. They are a record of the past. If you're overweight, if you're broke, if you're lonely—that's just a score that reflects your past thoughts, feelings, and habitual behaviors.

Your bank balance. Your romantic life. Your home. Your career. They are all just the outcome, the effects of what you've done or not done in the past. Whatever your results are right now, *they are just a scorecard.* If you don't like the scorecard, *you can change it by changing how you think, feel, and act.*

Change the roots, and you'll get different shoots. *That's* at the heart of Innercise.

Chapter Summary and Resources

Summary

- Change takes time. Actions you take *now* to change your brain plant seeds and spread roots for future harvests. Be patient.

- Building a daily Innercise ritual is crucial to your success.

- Typical components of Innercise rituals include relaxation/meditation, visualization using audio and video support, goal creation, specific training, and goal planning/review.

- Your current results are a scorecard of your past thoughts, feelings, and habitual behaviors. You can change your future scorecard by changing your brain starting today!

Additional Free Resources

If you want additional help and free resources on how to best use each section in the book, I'm including some special coaching videos and 9 mini brain-training audios to go along with the book. I will act as your mindset coach as part of buying Innercise. For now, get started with this book and the free resources. Just scan the code below on your smartphone and log in to the NeuroGym platform or go to www.myneurogym.com/innercise to create a log in so you gain access to the free bonuses and resources.

You, the Final Frontier

"All of us are guinea pigs in the laboratory of God.
Humanity is just a work in progress."

—Tennessee Williams

It's July 2017, and I've traveled to San Francisco to watch a brain at work.

I'm in the lab of Adam Gazzaley, MD, PhD. He's a professor at UC San Francisco, the founding director of the Neuroscience Imaging Center, and director of the Gazzaley Lab. It's the latter that's brought me here, and what I'm seeing is like something straight out of science fiction.

It's called the Glass Brain. On an enormous screen in front of me, a 3D computer image of a milky white brain hovers in space, rotating slowly, its folds and canyons clearly visible. Then, with a click, the image becomes transparent—like glass, as the name suggests.[36]

Inside the glasslike confines of the brain, colors flash and dance. There are bursts of yellow and green sparks, and colors that race across the interior of the brain in complex patterns. The various lobes glow pink at their outer edges, speckled with bright sparks of white. It's mesmerizing.

But these are more than just great special effects. This isn't just an image of a brain. This is an image of a real brain *working*. It's *his* brain—Gazzaley's—and the fireworks I'm witnessing are a real-time capture of the actual electrical impulses in his gray matter.

That's when it hits home: *I am watching Gazzaley think and feel as he's playing a video game.*

The science behind this is extraordinary. It requires some serious algorithmic mojo to take electrical impulses and turn them into a real-time moving light show. But Gazzaley's done it, and he thinks that combining this with video games and other therapies is the next breakthrough for a number of neural advancements.

To create the Glass Brain, you need to first capture the electrical information from the brain. Gazzaley and his team use a device that looks something like a swim cap covered in buttons. Each button is a sensor that captures electrical activity in the brain. From each sensor, a wire snakes across the room to a computer, where the data is stored and processed.

The whole process is a little Matrix-like—people connected at the head to giant supercomputers. But when you get out into the frontiers of neuroscience, one thing becomes abundantly clear. *The Matrix*—the mega-hit post-apocalyptic science-fiction film where everyone exists, at least mentally, in a virtual world created by computers—isn't nearly as futuristic as you might think.

A Short History of the Future of Brain Science

It's been a very long road to get to the Glass Brain. And from the perspective of the human brain itself, it's an even longer one. Imagine we travel back some 600 million years to a time when the earth is essentially a giant supercontinent, surrounded by a vast ocean. In that ocean floats what may be the common ancestor to all animals. It's a worm-like organism named *Urbilateria*. Some researchers believe that the first neural networks evolve in *Urbilateria*, and the rest of life flows from there.

Along the way, a lot happens. There are mass extinctions. The supercontinent breaks up. Later, another one forms. Then it breaks up too. There are ice ages. About 65 million years ago, a giant meteor slams into present-day Mexico, likely killing off the dinosaurs. But through it all, evolution continues, and, eventually, *homo sapiens* arise. That leads eventually to you, and the amazing brain that gives you…well, *you*.

The 10 Percent Rule: Myth or Mistaken Identity?

If you had to choose the most common "fact" about the brain that people think they know, this one would be a top contender:

Humans only use 5 to 10 percent of their brain.

It is, of course, wrong. The human brain is incredibly complex and we still struggle to fully understand it, but the idea that 90 percent of your brain is just wasted space is one thing we know *isn't* true.

Yet the idea is incredibly persistent. It was around when I was a kid, and I still hear it today. One study found that 65 percent of Americans still believe this to be true.[37] It's a neuro-myth.

Like many myths, however, I think it has something to teach us. Perhaps the reason it is so enduring is because in our reflective moments, when we can quiet our mind and escape the fears and anxieties that keep us stuck in the "matrix" of day-to-day life, we all face a powerful truth. We aren't missing out on using 90 percent of our brain; we're missing out on using 90 percent of our *potential*.

That's why the 10 percent myth endures—because we know that each one of us can achieve so much more than we do. We all have the ability to reach our goals and dreams. But we don't need to use *more* of our brain—rather, we need to use our brain *better*.

Sure, some parts of your brain are working harder than others at any given time. But 90 percent of your brain isn't useless filler. Magnetic resonance imaging shows that most of the human brain is active most of the time. In the course of a day, you use just about every part of your brain. The actual truth is that we use virtually all of our brain every day!

Innercise isn't about accessing some secret, dusty portion of the brain that the rest of the world is using and you aren't. It's about using your brain to help you reach your highest potential.

What's Next?

The evolution of our amazing brain continues. In the past 1.2 million years, for example, the human brain size has *doubled*. What's next? If we could travel forward in time from here, what would we find?

One thing we can be sure of is that brain evolution from here is going to take a unique path forward, one that mixes with technology in ways that will challenge everything we know about cognition, evolution, consciousness, and even *reality*. What the future holds for the brain is going to redefine what we think humans are capable of.

The Glass Brain is a peek into that and begs an answer to the question: "What's next?" Here's a glimpse:

- Passing energy through the brain, once the purview of early psychiatry and brain research, is now available to anyone with $100 and a willingness to strap a device to their head in search of everything from greater creativity and better focus to relief from depression. With transcranial direct current stimulation (TDCS), you can improve your focus, language and math skills, memory, and more.

- Trying to improve and reach your goals faster? Instead of the old way of getting a book, going to a seminar, or watching a video, the future of "do-it-yourself" brain training may come in the form of pills or neural devices.

- Planning a visit to Paris? Wouldn't it be great to learn French before you go? With the right neural stimulation, and improved technology to map your brain as you learn, you'll one day be able to speed up your ability to learn, consolidate new information and memories faster, and, like Keanu Reeves, learn new skills simply by "plugging in" to an educational virtual reality matrix.

- Troublesome emotional blocks and childhood traumas? As researchers zero in on the actual neural patterns for specific memories and emotions, we could develop the ability to "delete" or change them.

- Want a better brain? Researchers, neurohackers, and entrepreneurs are now studying and using psychedelics such as psilocybin, LSD, and MDMA for improving creativity, learning, and concentration, and for treating mental illnesses like depression and anxiety.

- What if instead of a pill or a therapist, you could just repair your own brain? Using neurofeedback—in essence, seeing your own brain in action—from fMRI or EEG technology, for example, you can observe your own brain activity, and use that information to change the way you think and feel. It's already showing promise for depression and ADHD, and many researchers believe that's just the tip of the treatment iceberg.

- Worried about Alzheimer's or dementia? As we get better at mapping brain activity, we'll be able to identify problematic brain lobes and regions before they become an issue. And then? We can repair or enhance them.

- Want to live in the Matrix? Virtual, augmented, and mixed reality is becoming…well, a reality. Companies are using software and high-tech eyewear to create immersive visual experiences, and haptic devices to provide physical feedback alongside it. The result is incredibly real simulations. And when things get real enough for your senses, they become real enough for the brain. We can now use VR to treat phobias, try extreme sports, and even switch genders. Add enough sensors and programming and a direct brain connection, and suddenly *The Matrix* isn't quite so far-fetched after all.

- Want to be bionic? More than forty years after the epic '70s show *The Six-Million Dollar Man* told the story of a crashed test pilot who's surgically rebuilt with high-tech legs, an arm, and an eye, we're now *actually giving people high-tech legs, arms, and even eyes*. The LUKE arm, for example, which can let users do things as delicate as handle chopsticks, is now being distributed to US Veterans. Muscle and brain-controlled prosthetics are now real.

- And the things we can't build, we'll grow. Scientists are now growing brain cells and even miniature brains! And not only can we grow them, we might just be able to *store* brains and bring them back again. Eternal life, anyone? Scientists have managed to successfully freeze and reanimate a mammal brain, opening the door a little wider to the possibility of cryogenics working at both ends of the spectrum. (Currently you can have your brain frozen, but only by signing off on the fact that no one knows if they'll ever be able to successfully *un*-freeze it.) If we can safely freeze and unfreeze your brain, living forever just got very, very real.

And that's assuming we even *need* a physical brain in order to live forever. I say that not to tease with absurdity, but with recognition that with faster than brain-level computing power just years away, and computer graphics cards that allow you to be in virtual reality and not know what is real and what isn't anymore, it may not be long until we can *actually duplicate a brain* in the form of software and hardware and even load and connect our brains onto a computer internet interface and experience a world beyond our wildest dreams. If we can digitize and connect brains, we can upload everyone to the cloud.

Some researchers even believe that within a decade we'll have AI (artificial intelligence) that's smarter than us and can display emotions. Within decades after that, we may be able to effectively *merge* with that intelligence, and that opens a gateway into a world that's almost impossible to conceive of, where we can interact with long-dead loved ones who've been re-created, and, in theory, change the nature of *consciousness*.

We are, in effect, on the brink of *changing what it means to be human*. From cyborgs to eternal life, much of what was considered the surreal is fast approaching the real—all thanks to our ability to understand and interact with our own brains.

The Here and Now: Deliberate Conscious Evolution

None of that, of course, is going to show up on your kitchen counter just yet. And while the future of goal achievement might involve taking a neuro-pill or having new knowledge, skills, and abilities implanted directly into your brain, the immediate promise of neuroplasticity and changing your brain offers more than enough amazing future for all of us.

Innercise is one technology that's available now, that works, and that can change your life.

But it has one requirement: *your commitment.*

Thirty-five years ago, in a Toronto restaurant my mentor Alan Brown asked me if I was interested in, or if I was *committed* to, achieving my goals. His question—and my answer—changed the course of my life.

That same question is before you now. The frontiers of brain science and the practical here-and-now success of Innercise tell us is that change is *possible.* Yes, it may be hard. Yes, you're going to experience discomfort and relapses. Yes, you'll face challenges. But the lesson of Innercise is this: *You are in the driver's seat.*

With your conscious effort, you can deliberately gain more control over the direction of your life. You can go from "hopium" and "excusitis" to *creating the life of your dreams.*

You—yes, *you*—can take the remaining time you have left on this beautiful blue planet and do what I believe we are each here for: to trade your time for what will give you the most meaning, what will offer you your highest purpose, and what will best share your gifts to inspire as many others as you possibly can.

To your success,

John Assaraf
CEO, Founder NeuroGym
2018

Getting Help

NeuroGym is the world's leading provider of scientifically proven methods, tools, and resources to help people strengthen their mindset and upgrade their emotional skills, so they achieve their goals faster and easier than ever before.

Our team of neuroscientists, researchers, psychologists, and high performance organizational experts are committed to bringing you cutting-edge scientific findings, methods, tools, and resources to maximize your potential.

Just like a coach, therapist, or psychologist might guide you through a specialized mindset or emotional fortitude training process, you can use **our live coaching and on-demand training platform to learn science-based methods to strengthen your mindset and skills, so you achieve your biggest goals and dreams faster and easier than ever before.**

If you'd like to go deeper and further than the Innercises in this book, visit www.myneurogym.com/innercise to get started.

NeuroGym Programs

NeuroGym applies scientifically-proven methods and technologies for helping people expand their mental and emotional power to reach their fullest potential. More than 100,000 people have used NeuroGym programs like

Winning the Game of Money
Automatically retrain your brain to have the beliefs, habits, confidence, perceptions, and behaviors of a multimillionaire.

Winning the Game of Weight Loss
Reset your brain's fat set point and hidden self-image by utilizing the latest evidence-based technologies and methodologies from Cognitive Neuroscience and Psychology.

Winning the Game of Fear
Eliminate debilitating fears, emotions, doubts, anxieties, stress, or worries. Develop unstoppable confidence and the beliefs and habits to quickly achieve your goals and live the life you deserve.

Having It All
Identify your true innermost goals and create an unshakeable road map for achieving them. Discover the seven natural laws that will make it easier than ever before as you retrain the way you think, act, and achieve.

The Neuroscience of Predictable Business Growth and Profits
Discover with absolute precision your best sales and marketing strategies for exponential growth and profits in your business.

To learn more about our programs and technologies, visit www. MyNeuroGym.com.

Master List of Innercises

To download a master reference list of Innercises, including instructions and my guidance for each, go to

www.myneurogym.com/innercise.

To sign up for our free Brain-A-Thon training with me and other world-renowned brain and success experts, visit www. innercisebook.com/brainathon

Acknowledgments

For the last thirty-seven years, I have learned and applied almost every tool, technology, and technique to manage my emotions and get my mindset right. My early mentors wrote and were referenced in the hundreds of books I read and the audios I listened to.

In the past ten years though, I have taken an even deeper dive into the world of neuroscience and neuropsychology. Thus, I want to deeply thank several amazing friends and mentors who have been particularly influential in helping shape my understanding of the human brain, and who have truly made this book possible.

Mark Robert Waldman has been relentless in keeping me on the right track of "real" brain science and far away from pseudoscience. His constant fact-checking, teaching, editing, and research has been irreplaceable.

Dr. Srini Pillay, whose genius and never-ending search for ways to explain the complexities of the brain and mind have taken me to depths of knowledge I had no idea I was capable of understanding. Dr. Joan Rosenberg schooled me on the vast world of emotions and how to maximize their power in day-to-day life. Dr. Daniel Amen, whose understanding of nuclear psychiatry and brain imaging has deepened my quest to consistently learn more and raise up my game.

A very special thanks to Dan Clements who helped me write this book. He watched me wrestle for over a year with my own fears and insecurities of writing what I worried would not end up on par with what I know could help people versus what I could articulate on paper. A big thank-you to Kenneth Kales who tirelessly helped me edit this book. Your outstanding suggestions truly took it to the next level. Also, my assistants Kimberly and Ashley have been invaluable in dealing with my schedule and in helping me manage the hundreds of moving parts to create this book while running NeuroGym. Thank you so much!

Maria, my life partner, is a never-ending source of love and inspiration. She gives me every possible reason and opportunity to be the best me possible. And to our sons, Keenan and Noah, the depth of my love for you is impossible for me to express in words. I am so completely proud of you and deeply love you and who you are. My brother Marc and sister Rivka, all I can say is WOW! I feel blessed and grateful to be on this amazing life journey with you. Thank you. I love you. I appreciate you.

And to GOD, my deepest gratitude for making all things possible.

Endnotes

1   Fields, R. Douglas. 2014. "Myelin - More than Insulation." *Science.* New York, NY: PMC, April 18. https://www.ncbi.nlm.nih.gov/pmc/articles/PMC5017201/.

2   Merzenich, Michael M., Thomas M. Van Vleet, and Mor Nahum. 2014. *Brain Plasticity-Based Therapeutics.* June 27. Accessed January 2018. https://www.ncbi.nlm.nih.gov/pmc/articles/PMC4072971/.

3   Kidd, Celeste, and Y. Benjamin Hayden. 2015. "The Psychology and Neuroscience of Curiosity." *Neuron* 88 (3): 449-460. https://www.cell.com/neuron/fulltext/S0896-6273(15)00767-9.

4   Joensson, Morten, Kristine Romer Thomsen, Lau M. Andersen, Joachim Gross, Kim Mouridsen, Kristian Sandberg, Leid Ostergaard, and Hans C. Lou. 2015. "Making sense: Dopamine activates conscious self-monitoring through medial prefrontal cortex." *Human Brain Mapping* 36(5): 1866-1877. https://www.ncbi.nlm.nih.gov/pmc/articles/PMC4737196/

5   Davidson, Richard J., and Antoine Lutz. 2008. "Buddha's Brain: Neuroplasticity and Meditation." *EEE signal processing magazine* 25.1: 174-176. https://www.ncbi.nlm.nih.gov/pmc/articles/PMC2944261/.

6   Keng, Shian-Ling, Moria J. Smoski, and Clive J. Robins. 2011. "Effects of Mindfulness on Psychological Health: A Review of Empirical Studies." *Clinical Psychology Review* 31.6: 1041-1056. https://www.ncbi.nlm.nih.gov/pmc/articles/PMC3679190/.

7   Sayal, Natasha. 2015. "Exercise training increases size of hippocampus and improves memory PNAS." *Annals of Neurosciences* 108 (7): 3017-3022. https://www.ncbi.nlm.nih.gov/pmc/articles/PMC4480257/.

8   Newberg M.D., Andrew, and Mark Robert Waldman. 2016. *How Enlightenment Changes Your Brain: The New Science of Transformation.* Avery.

9   Newberg, Andrew B. 2014. "The Neuroscientific Study of Spiritual Practices." *Frontiers in Psychology* 5: 215. https://www.ncbi.nlm.nih.gov/pmc/articles/PMC3957224/

10 Kappes, Heather Barry, and Gabriele Oettingen. 2011. "Positive Fantasies about Idealized Futures Sap Energy." *Journal of Experimental Social Psychology* 47 (4).

11 Pascual-Leone, A., D. Nguyet, L.G. Cohen, J.P. Brasil-Neto, A. Cammarota, and M. Hallett. 1995. "Modulation of muscle responses evoked by transcranial magnetic stimulation during the acquisition of new fine motor skills." *Journal of Neurophysiology* 74 (3): 1037-1045. https://www.ncbi.nlm.nih.gov/pubmed/7500130.

12 Fogg, BJ. n.d. *Tiny Habits.* http://tinyhabits.com.

13 Clear, James. n.d. "How to Build New Habits by Taking Advantage of Old Ones." *James Clear.* How to Build New Habits by Taking Advantage of Old Ones. http://jamesclear.com/habit-stacking

14 Sethi, Maneesh, interview by Dave Asprey. 2018. *Gaming Your Habits* (April 24). https://blog.bulletproof.com/maneesh-sethi/

15   Waldman, Mark Robert, and Chris Manning. 2017. *NeuroWisdom: The New Brain Science of Money, Happiness, and Success.* Diversion Books.

16   Waldman, Mark Robert, and Chris Manning. 2017. *NeuroWisdom: The New Brain Science of Money, Happiness, and Success.* Diversion Books.

17   Crum, Alia J., and Ellen J. Langer. 2007. "Mind-set Matters: Exercise and the Placebo Effect." *Psychological Science* 18 (2): 165-171. https://dash.harvard.edu/ bitstream/handle/1/3196007/Langer_ExcersisePlaceboEffect.pdf

18   Hsu, Laura M., Jaewoo Chung, and Ellen J. Langer. 2010. "The Influence of Age-Related Cues on Health and Longevity." *Perspectives of Psychological Science* 5 (6): 632-648. http://pps.sagepub.com/content/5/6/632.abstract.

19   Achor, Shawn. 2011. *Harvard Business Review.* February 15. https://hbr. org/2011/02/make-stress-work-for-you;.

20   Levy, Becca R., Martin D. Slade, Suzanne R. Kunkel, and Stanislav V. Kasl. 2002. "Longevity Increased by Positive Self-Perceptions of Aging." *Journal of Personality and Social Psychology* 83 (2): 261-270. http://www.apa.org/pubs/journals/releases/ psp-832261.pdf.

21   Mangels, Jennifer A., Brady Butterfield, Justin Lamb, Catherine Good, and Carol S. Dweck. 2006. "Why do beliefs about intelligence influence learning success? A social cognitive neuroscience model." *Social Cognitive and Affective Neuroscience* 75-86. https://www.ncbi.nlm.nih.gov/pmc/articles/PMC1838571/.

22   Andrews-Hanna, Jessica R., Jonathan Smallwood, and R. Nathan Spreng. 2014. "The default network and self-generated thought: component processes, dynamic control, and clinical relevance." *The Year in Cognitive Neuroscience* 1316 (1): 29-52. https://nyaspubs.onlinelibrary.wiley.com/doi/abs/10.1111/nyas.12360

23   Mrazek, Michael D., Michael S. Franklin, Dawa Tarchin Phillips, Benjamin Baird, and Jonathan W. Schooler. 2013. "Mindfulness Training Improves Working Memory Capacity and GRE Performance While Reducing Mind Wandering ." *Psychological Science* 24 (5): 776-781. http://pss.sagepub.com/content/24/5/776.

24   Brewer, Judson. 2011. "Meditation experience is associated with differences in default mode network activity and connectivity." *Proceedings of the National Academy of Sciences of the United States of America.* http://www.ncbi.nlm.nih.gov/ pubmed/22114193.

25   Holzel, Britta K. 2011. "Mindfulness practice leads to increases in regional brain gray matter density." *Psychiatry Research* 36-43. https://www.ncbi.nlm.nih.gov/ pmc/articles/PMC3004979/

26   Menon, Vinod, and Lucina Q. Uddin. 2010. "Saliency, switching, attention and control: a network model of insula function." *Brain Structure & Function* 655-667. https://www.ncbi.nlm.nih.gov/pmc/articles/PMC2899886/\

27   Crum, Alia J., and Ellen J. Langer. 2007. "Mind-set Matters: Exercise and the Placebo Effect." *Psychological Science* 18 (2): 165-171. https://mbl.stanford.edu/ sites/default/files/crum_rethinkingstress_jpsp_2013.pdf

28   Hanson, Rick. n.d. "Confronting Negativity Bias." *Rick Hanson.* http://www. rickhanson.net/how-your-brain-makes-you-easily-intimidated/.

29   Anderson, Nancy L. n.d. "5 Ways To Make Your New Years Resolutions Stick." *Forbes.* https://www.forbes.com/sites/financialfinesse/2013/01/03/5-ways-to-make-your-new-years-resolutions-stick/#7ae58d011ebd.

30   Comaford, Christine. 2015. "Achieve Your Goals Faster: The Latest Neuroscience Of Goal Attainment." *Forbes.* November 22. https://www.forbes.com/sites/ christinecomaford/2015/11/22/achieve-your-goals-faster-the-latest-neuroscience- of-goal-attainment/#15755966e25d.

31   G. Oettingen and B. Schwörer, "Mind Wandering via Mental Contrasting as a Tool for Behavior Change," *Front Psychol* 4 (Sep 2, 2013):0 562; D. T. Stuss, "Functions of the Frontal Lobes: Relation to Executive Functions," *J Int Neuropsychol* Soc 17, no. 5 (Sep 2011): 759–65; and A. T. Sevincer, P. D. Busatta, and G. Oettingen, "Mental Contrasting and Transfer of Energization," *Pers Soc Psychol Bull* 40, no. 2 (Feb 2014): 139–52.

32   Oettingen, Gabriele, and Doris Mayer. 2002. "The motivating function of thinking about the future: Expectations versus fantasies." *Journal of Personality and Social Psychology* 83 (5): 1198-1212. https://www.ncbi.nlm.nih.gov/ pubmed/12416922

33   Milne, S., S. Orbell, and P. Sheeran. 2002. "Combining motivational and volitional interventions to promote exercise participation: protection motivation theory and implementation intentions." *British Journal of Health Psychology* 7 (Pt.2): 163-184. https://www.ncbi.nlm.nih.gov/pubmed/14596707

34   Robert P. Spunt, Emily B. Falk, and Matthew D. Lieberman, "Dissociable Neural Systems Support Retrieval of How and Why Action Knowledge," *Psychological Science* 21 (2010): 1593, originally published online 19 October 2010, DOI: 10.1177/0956797610386618.

35   Lally, Phillippa, Cornelia Jaarsveld, Henry Potts, and Jane Wardle. 2010. "How are habits formed: Modelling habit formation in the real world." *European Journal of Social Psychology* 40: 998-1009. https://centrespringmd.com/docs/How%20 Habits%20are%20Formed.pdf

36   You can see the Glass Brain at https://www.youtube.com/watch?v=dAIQeTeMJ-I.

37   Robynne Boyd, "Do People Only Use 10 Percent Of Their Brains?," *Scientific American*, February 7, 2008, https://www.scientificamerican.com/article/ do-people-only-use-10-percent-of-their-brains/